QUIET

Prayer Interludes for Women

SPACES

PATRICIA WILSON

UPPER
ROOM BOOKS®
NASHVILLE

QUIET SPACES: Prayer Interludes for Women
© 2002 by Patricia F. Wilson
All rights reserved.

Upper Room® Web site: http://www.upperroom.org

THE UPPER ROOM®, UPPER ROOM BOOKS®, and design logos are trademarks owned by The Upper Room®, Nashville, Tennessee. All rights reserved.

Unless otherwise indicated, scriptures are taken from the HOLY BIBLE, NEW INTERNATIONAL VERSION. Copyright 1973, 1978, 1984 by International Bible Society. Used by permission of Zondervan Publishing House. All rights reserved.

Scriptures marked NRSV are taken from the New Revised Standard Version Bible, copyright 1989, Division of Christian Education of the National Council of the Churches of Christ in the United States of America. Used by permission. All rights reserved.

Cover and interior design: Ed Maksimowicz
Cover illustration: Morning Scene © O'Brien Productions/
  CORBIS
Second printing: 2002
Printed in the United States of America

Library of Congress Cataloging-in-Publication Data
Wilson, Patricia, 1943–
Quiet spaces: prayer interludes for women / by Patricia Wilson.
    p. cm
ISBN 0-8358-0969-2
    1. Women—Prayer-books and devotions—English. I. Title.
BV4527. W558 2001
242'.843—dc21   2001045439

For all the prayer partners,
fellowship groups,
and caring friends who
have brought me to
this place of faith

Contents

A QUIET SPACE
to Pray for Life's Stresses

A Quiet Space
to Pray for a Relationship

A Quiet Space
to Celebrate Special Occasions

A QUIET SPACE
for Endings and Beginnings

Introduction

In today's world, women are busier than ever. Not only does a woman often manage the multiple tasks and responsibilities of home, family, and career, but she also juggles a variety of roles—mother, daughter, wife, employee, friend, volunteer—the list seems endless. Each morning she hits the ground running, to-do list in hand and pocket planner held aloft. By the time the last minutes of the day drain away, she falls into an exhausted sleep, haunted by the ghosts of things yet to do.

How can a busy woman find time for personal prayer during one hectic day after another? How can God speak to her amidst the turbulence of timetables, schedules, and agendas? Where is a moment for her to hear God's still small voice above the tumult?

Is this your challenge—finding time to pray? Believe it or not, time for prayer is available to you through the Bowling Ball Solution.

Imagine that your day is like an empty cardboard box about two feet square. This box contains all the waking time available to you in a day. Your most important to-do items—writing a business report, going to the doctor, meeting with your child's teacher, shopping for the week's groceries—are like bowling balls. They are large, bulky, inflexible blocks of time.

How many of these will fit into your box? About four? Now your day is full of important things to do.

What about the spaces between the bowling balls? You have room for a few tennis balls—things that take a little less time than your major projects but still have to get done: returning a library book, dropping off the dry cleaning, picking up milk on the way home. These tennis balls of time soon fill up the spaces around your bowling balls.

A little space remains, however. You can put in a few golf balls—those unplanned half hours of time here and there when meetings start late, new work comes in, or a meeting runs overtime.

Your time box is now full. There's no room for anything else, much less room for your personal prayer time!

Now in your mind's eye see grains of sand. How many you can pour into the box before it's completely filled? Quite a few!

The grains of sand are stray minutes of unassigned time. They usually go unnoticed and unused. Where do they come from?

You can find these stray minutes while you are on hold with that government department, sitting in the waiting room at the dentist's office, stopped in a traffic jam, on a short coffee break, waiting for a meeting to begin, between phone calls—in any one of the myriad times during the day when a small opportunity of time opens up. These "quiet spaces" are all around you.

Quiet Spaces is a book of just such times— short interludes of time as little as five minutes each—that you can capture and use to touch the hand of God. Each Quiet Space has five components:

1. *Calming:* a passage from the Psalms to calm your mind.
2. *Centering:* an exercise to focus your thoughts.
3. *Praying:* a prayer for the particular Quiet Space.
4. *Listening:* a Gospel passage offering the words of Jesus.
5. *Returning:* an exercise to anchor your prayer experience.

Whenever you have a Quiet Space, take the opportunity to spend those few minutes with God. Read through the passage from Psalms (under Calming) three times, which will help calm your mind and heart. If you wish, you may write the psalm on an index card and leave it where it you can see it during the day.

Next, focus your thoughts with a moment of imagination. The Centering suggestions will give you an idea of how to do this. You don't have to close your eyes.

Now read through the short prayer. Read it slowly, paying attention to the words. The short sentences and thoughts of Quiet Space prayers help you do this. If you find your mind wandering, start over at the beginning and read through again. Where you see italicized words in the prayer, substitute the name, gender, or situation of your own personal prayer.

When you finish the prayer, read the words of Jesus (under Listening). Consider how they relate to your life and your present situation. Quietly thank Jesus for his love and care.

Then anchor your experience and prepare to return to your world by using the Returning exercise. Sometimes you can continue to use this exercise throughout the day to remind you of the Quiet Space.

These Quiet Spaces can take as little as five minutes. If you have time, you can spend a few quiet minutes after each section thinking about what God is saying to you.

This book contains many Quiet Spaces, divided into various prayer subjects. Whether you choose to read them in sequence, randomly, or by topic, God is waiting to speak to you in the Quiet Space. 🙺

A QUIET
SPACE
to Find
Refreshment

When You Feel Tired and Worn-Out

CALMING

You are awesome, O God, in your sanctuary;
    the God of Israel gives power and strength
        to his people.

PSALM 68:35

CENTERING

Take three deep breaths. Slowly fill your lungs, hold each breath, and exhale after each one. As you do so, imagine taking in strength and power. Picture them filling your entire body.

PRAYING

Dear God, here I am before you. I'm tired—so tired. I keep wondering what happened to my

21

boundless enthusiasm for the life you've given me. Where did it go? When did I lose it?

In place of my enthusiasm, I feel dried out. Deadened.

I don't feel like your victorious child, God. Why has this happened to me? How did I let this happen? Why did you let it happen?

I know all the right things to say. I know that my strength lies in you, that without you I can do nothing. And yet, here I am, powerless, worn-out, and weak.

Let me feel your strength, O God—

- the power of your Holy Spirit filling my weary body,
- the energy of your love flowing through me,
- the joy of your salvation bubbling up from my heart.

Take my weariness, my fatigue, and my heaviness. Lift them from my spirit. Fill me with joy, enthusiasm, and zest for life and the tasks before me.

Help me to see every new day as a perfect gift from you, to be lived fully and powerfully, secure in the knowledge that you will provide me with the strength I need to do this.

(Take three more deep breaths, imagining that each one is bringing in energy and strength.)

Thank you, O God, for taking this weariness from me. Thank you for restoring my strength.

Listening

Come with me by yourselves to a quiet place and get some rest.

MARK 6:31

Returning

Take three more deep breaths, hold them for a few seconds, and slowly release them. Repeat this exercise throughout the day, each time imagining the strength of Jesus Christ filling and sustaining you.

When You Need to Feel God's Presence

CALMING
I call on you, O God, for you will answer me;
   give ear to me and hear my prayer.

PSALM 17:6

CENTERING
Imagine sitting in your favorite chair, waiting quietly for a friend to join you. You hear footsteps behind you and feel excitement and anticipation. You don't have to look up to know it is your friend.

PRAYING
Merciful and loving God, welcome to my quiet space. Thank you for coming when I called.

I need you right now.

I need to be with you.

I need to feel your touch.

I need to hear your voice.

So many things are happening, and I feel overwhelmed. So many people want my time.

I have so many demands to meet, so many promises to keep.

I feel as if I've lost you in the midst of everything around me. And so, I sit quietly now and welcome your presence here with me.

Speak to me, O God, in this brief space. Slow my anxious thoughts, still my pounding heart, calm my fears and doubts.

Tell me that you love me and care for me.

Remind me that I am your child and I don't have to be afraid or overwhelmed.

Touch me, God, in this moment. Let me feel your hand upon me, your love pouring over me, your comforting Holy Spirit all around me.

Give me an awareness of your loving presence in this quiet space.

Thank you, my Lord, that all I have to do is ask, and you are here. Thank you for always being with me, for always waiting for me to stop, pray, and listen.

Thank you for your ever-present love.

Keep me in your presence today, O Lord, no matter what befalls me.

LISTENING

The kingdom of God does not come with your careful observation, nor will people say, "Here it is," or "There it is," because the kingdom of God is within you.

LUKE 17:20-21

RETURNING

Sit quietly in the awareness that God is with you. Feel yourself wrapped in God's love and peace. Sense the Holy Spirit permeating your body and overflowing in a sense of joy. Thank God for being with you today.

When You Feel
You've Lost Your Way

Calming

Hear my prayer, O LORD;
   let my cry for help come to you.
Do not hide your face from me
   when I am in distress.
Turn your ear to me;
   when I call, answer me quickly.

PSALM 102:1-2

Centering

The Shepherd knows his sheep, and they know his voice. Imagine Jesus' voice gently calling you, lovingly whispering your name in your ear. Jesus calls to you personally because he knows you and your needs even before you speak.

Thank you, Gentle Shepherd, for being here with me at this moment. Jesus, my Shepherd who watches over me and cares for me, I feel like a lost sheep searching for the sheepfold.

I don't know how I lost my way. Perhaps in the busyness of my life, I've forgotten how to follow the Shepherd:

to keep my eyes on you,

   to keep my thoughts on you,

      to keep my ears open to your voice.

Instead, I've gotten caught up in the things of this world. Like a lost sheep, I stumble along the edges of high cliffs. I find myself sinking in the quicksand of hidden bogs. I hear the howling of my enemies during the watches of the dark night. I rush around, trying to find my own way out.

But instead of finding you in my blind activity, I am even further from you.

And I am afraid.

(Imagine that you can hear the voice of Jesus calling your name again.)

I hear you, my Shepherd. In this moment, Jesus, I will be very still. I will wait for you to find me. I will stop talking, stop rushing, stop doing, and just wait.

(Sit silently for a minute.)

Your presence is all around me. Your gentle hand guides me back to the fold. I feel safe, peaceful, and home at last.

Thank you, Gentle Shepherd.

LISTENING

I am the good shepherd; I know my sheep and my sheep know me—just as the Father knows me and I know the Father—and I lay down my life for the sheep.

JOHN 10:14-15

RETURNING

Take a moment and feel the caring love of Jesus fill the air around you. Hear his voice calling your name. As the day goes on, if you find yourself beginning to rush and hurry, stand still, be still, and wait for the Shepherd to find you.

When You Feel Alone and Forgotten

Calming

He brought them out of darkness and gloom,
    and broke their bonds asunder.
Let them thank the Lord for his steadfast love,
    for his wonderful works to humankind.

Psalm 107:14-15, NRSV

Centering

Imagine standing on a vast beach that stretches for miles in each direction, facing a calm, flat, empty ocean that flows into the horizon. You are alone. No birds are overhead; you do not hear the sound of waves, nor do you feel the wind blowing. Experience the sense of being completely alone.

PRAYING

Here I stand, O my God, alone.

    Have you forgotten me?

I feel so far away from you,

    from other people,

        from the world.

    I am alone.

How did I get here, in this lonely place? When did I lose that sense of your presence near me? Who moved?

    I try to tell myself that this is just a bad

        patch,

            that I'm tired,

                that too many things are going on

                    in my life,

                        that everything will be as it

                  was—

if I just hang in there.

But I'm tired of just hanging in there and hoping that you and I will connect. I don't like feeling disjointed, uneasy, empty.

    I am alone.

Where are you, God? How do I find you again? Where do I have to go? What do I have to do? I don't have any answers, and I can't hear your voice in my loneliness.

I long for the way it used to be: when I could feel your touch, your presence near me. How did I get lost?

Perhaps this is one of those times I will just have to walk in faith. God, here are three things I know:

- that you love me,
- that you have a plan for me,
- and that you are with me.

Even though I know those things, I don't *feel* them. If I did, I wouldn't be here now, telling you that I feel alone.

But I know those things because in the past, they were absolutely true. Just because I can't feel them now doesn't mean they're no longer true.

So, God, I'm going to begin a faith walk with you. I will believe that these three things are still true:

- that you love me,
- that you have a plan for me,
- and that you are with me.

Even if I feel alone.

I offer you my faith walk. Please be with me, encourage and strengthen me, so that one day, maybe soon, I won't feel alone anymore.

LISTENING

I will not leave you as orphans; I will come to you.

JOHN 14:18

RETURNING

Imagine yourself on the beach again. Look down the beach. In the distance, you see a figure beckoning to you. See yourself walking toward the figure—toward Jesus, who is waiting for you.

When You Need
Peace and Quiet

CALMING

But I have stilled and quieted my soul;
  like a weaned child with its mother,
  like a weaned child is my soul within me.

PSALM 131:2

CENTERING

Wherever you are right now, imagine putting up sound barriers all around you. These barriers are invisible, stretching from the ground to the outer atmosphere. No sound, no people, no outside intrusions can penetrate these barriers. You can put the barriers just a foot away from yourself or surround a larger space—whichever feels most comfortable. Within the barriers, all

is silent and peaceful. Sit within your imaginary
barriers for a moment.

Praying

It's unusual for me to feel peaceful and quiet,
dear Jesus, because there is always so much
noise, so much confusion, so much other stuff
going on all around me.

People demanding my time,
  projects demanding my attention,
    tasks demanding my effort.

I long for a place with sound barriers: a place
where I can go to be quiet, where I can find the
peace that is missing from my life.

I know that you often felt the same way—
that you had the same need to find a place away
from everything where you could rest and be
quiet. You didn't seem to find it any easier to do
that than I do, and you are the Son of God,
with legions of angels at your command!

How I need a place of peace in my life, dear
Jesus, a place just for us.

No one else but me and you. There we
would be, just the two of us.

No one interrupting us with their
  complaints and demands.

No phones ringing, televisions blaring,
or traffic roaring.

No deadlines, no alarm clocks,
no schedules.

Nothing else. Just me and you.

As I talk to you, Christ Jesus, I'm beginning to realize that in this talking is a peace. As I concentrate on what I'm saying to you and listen for the sound of your voice, I'm beginning to shut out all the noise around me.

Our communion with each other is erecting barriers all around. The world outside me fades, the sounds die down, and I can finally relax in this quiet space.

Here we are, resting in each other's presence. Just me and you.

I thank you, Christ Jesus, for this small space of peace and quiet with you. I thank you that this space is always here, always waiting for me, and in these few moments, I can find the refreshing that I need.

That's all it takes—a few moments with you. A few moments of peace and quiet.

Just me and you.

Listening

Peace I leave with you; my peace I give you. I do not give to you as the world gives. Do not let your hearts be troubled and do not be afraid.

JOHN 14:27

Returning

Continue to sit for a few moments, enjoying your quiet space. Then, one by one, take down your invisible barriers and return to your world. Remember that the quiet space is always there, always available to you when you feel the need for peace and quiet.

When You Need Encouragement

CALMING

Though the LORD is on high, he looks upon the
   lowly,
   but the proud he knows from afar.
Though I walk in the midst of trouble,
   you preserve my life;
you stretch out your hand against the anger
   of my foes,
with your right hand you save me.

PSALM 138:6-7

CENTERING

In your mind, picture a high, rocky cliff. You are
climbing up that cliff. Your goal is to reach the
plateau at the top, where you know that the

38

view is wonderful. You're about halfway up, and climbing has become really difficult. In fact, you've reached a spot where you feel you can't go on. You don't want to go back down and miss the view from the top. You can't stay where you are. You just need a little help to go on.

PRAYING

I'm tired of "keeping on keeping on," God. Every day is like climbing up that cliff—hard, lonely work. I just want to give up.

I'm not sure what I want to give up—

    the climb,

        the goal,

            the effort,

                the relentless pressing on,

                the discouragement,

                the pain,

                    the disappointment, or

                    the frustration.

I just know that right now the goal seems so far away that I forget why I began climbing.

Most of the time I feel like I'm the only one climbing. My fellow travelers seem to have taken a different route—perhaps their way is easier, or maybe they're just better climbers. But

I'm struggling, O God, and I need help.

The cliff is so high and so hard. There are so many rocky places where I can't get a firm grip. Some places are slippery and treacherous. Others seem easy until I get there, and then they're not easy at all but just as treacherous as the places I left behind me.

I know that this cliff must be part of your plan for my life, God, but that doesn't make it any easier right now. It's still a hard climb, and I'm tired.

O God, help me today. Give me the courage to continue in this path. Help me over the rocky spots, the slippery places, the difficult passes. I can't do this alone.

Maybe that's been my problem all along—I've been trying to climb by myself. I forgot why I'm climbing in the first place—to enjoy the view from the top.

God, right now I place this climb in your hands. I give up. I will allow you to bring me the rest of the way, even to carry me if need be. Together we can make this climb. Thank you, my Lord, for being with me.

LISTENING

No one who puts a hand to the plow and looks back is fit for the kingdom of God.

LUKE 9:62, NRSV

RETURNING

Imagine that you are still stuck on your cliff. Now imagine a hand reaching down, grasping yours, and pulling you upward. The climb becomes easier, much easier, and that strong hand—the hand of God—is always present, guiding you, holding you, carrying you, as you continue the climb up your cliff.

When Joy Is Missing from Your Life

CALMING

Bring joy to your servant,
for to you, O Lord,
I lift up my soul.

PSALM 86:4

CENTERING

Imagine a fountain in a park. The fountain appears not to have worked for a long time. Its basin is dry and filled with leaves.

PRAYING

O God, my joy has dried up. Nothing is left inside me—none of the flowing, bubbling, splashing joy I used to have. And I am dry.

My life is empty—arid, barren, devoid of color. I simply exist, joyless and sorrowing.

I long for what I remember so well: those moments of pure happiness when I looked on my world and saw all the good in it.

I long for the singing joy that was always within me, a gift from you.

This joyless life isn't what Jesus promised me. He promised that he came so that my joy would be full. And it was, at the beginning. I can remember what life was like when the grass was greener and the sky was bluer; I saw you, God, in everything and everyone around me. I lived my life then—fully and completely.

Now I simply exist.

I want your promise. I want your joy—full, flowing, and never ending. I want to feel light and happy, glad to be alive and glad to be a Christian.

So I ask you now, O God, to fulfill your promise to me. Release the springs of joy within me. Let them flow so strongly and surely that my doubts and fears are washed away, swept up in the waters of your joy.

Let that joy flow out of me to those around me, bubbling over, spreading out, and covering all the barren ground of my life. Make me a wellspring of joy for others whose lives need the waters of your love.

Thank you, God, that even when I feel empty and dry, I know that the springs of joy are there, buried deep within me. I ask you to tap those springs now, release them, and carry me away on their fullness.

Thank you, O God, for joy.

Joy that overcomes all else.

Joy that is more powerful than the darkest powers.

Joy that is more abundant than the waters in the seas.

Joy that is mine.

LISTENING

I have told you this so that my joy may be in you and that your joy may be complete.

JOHN 15:11

RETURNING

Bring to mind again the image of the dry fountain. Now imagine the fountain suddenly bubbling up with water; the water is so abundant that it starts to leap up in dancing spouts. Water dances and splashes into the dry basin until it spills over the sides and spreads all around the fountain. Keep that image in your mind throughout the day. Remind yourself that God's joy waits within you, ready to be released so that you and those around you can be refreshed.

A QUIET
SPACE
to Offer
Thanksgiving

Thanks
for Your Home

CALMING

How lovely is your dwelling place,
  O LORD Almighty!
My soul yearns, even faints, for the courts of the
  LORD;
my heart and my flesh cry out for the living
  God.
Even the sparrow has found a home,
  and the swallow a nest for herself,
  where she may have her young—
a place near your altar, O LORD Almighty. . . .
Blessed are those who dwell in your house;
  they are ever praising you.

PSALM 84:1-4

CENTERING

Think of a place in your home where you feel happy. It might be the bedroom, the living room, or the kitchen. Think of this place, and bring it to your mind clearly. See it with all the detail you can put into it. Hold it close to you for a moment, and enjoy this place.

PRAYING

Thank you, Gracious God, for my home.

Thank you that even though your own son had no home, I have been blessed with this place to live. Thank you for these walls, this roof, these windows and doors.

Thank you so much for this part of my life. I know that material things are not important, that my real treasure is in heaven, but God, this place is a treasure to me.

As I look around my home, I think of other people who do not have walls like this, floors, ceilings, or a roof. I think of them, cold and shivering in the dark. I love my home, but my treasure isn't in my possessions, my special places, my home. I could leave them all if that's what you asked of me. Until you ask that, O God, I thank you for my home.

And in my gratitude, O God, I also offer you a prayer for the homeless of this world—

those across the sea,

in faraway lands,

in other nations,

and in my own backyard.

I don't know how to pray for these people, Gracious God. I suppose I'd like to ask you to give a home to each person. I know you can do this only through your people.

I am one of your people. Open my heart so that I can share my wealth and prosperity with others. Until I do that, O God, I ask you to touch those in need with your loving hand.

LISTENING

Truly I tell you, just as you did it to one of the least of these who are members of my family, you did it to me.

MATTHEW 25:40, NRSV

RETURNING

As you think about your home, lift up the homeless in prayer. When you are in your special place in your home, ask God to show you how to help the homeless persons around you.

Thanks
for Your Job

CALMING
You will eat the fruit of your labor;
blessings and prosperity will be yours.

PSALM 128:2

CENTERING
Think about your workplace. Then imagine the
scene changing. You are standing in a field of
ripe grain that is ready for the harvest. The field
is vast, stretching from horizon to horizon. You
are alone in this field.

PRAYING
Providing God, thank you for my job.
Because of this job I can pay my bills, feed

my family, and live my life. Because of this job, I have a purpose each day, a place to go, and work to do.

Thank you, God, for my job.

So many people would give anything to have my job because they don't have a job. They search day after day, hoping to find work. They stand in line at the unemployment office, feeling humiliated, outcast from the rest of us.

Thank you, God, for my job.

Sometimes I get tired of the people at work:
the whiners and complainers,
the naysayers and backstabbers,
the bullies and cheats.
Then I remember the others:
the saints and soldiers,
the peacemakers and cheerleaders,
the listeners and uplifters.
And I am thankful.

Sometimes getting to work every morning is a hassle. Day after day, month after month; the same place, the same people, the same work. Sometimes I get tired of it all and begin to wish that I didn't have this job. But then there are days when I love my job—the place, the people, and the work.

O God, thank you for my job.

Even when the work piles up.

Even when I'm faced with pressures, demands, and stresses—not enough time, not enough people, not enough resources—I thank you because I know that in you I have the strength to do all things.

Thank you for my job, God.

Thank you for the opportunity every day to show your face to those around me:

to my coworkers and my bosses,
to my employees and my customers,
to all those people I come in contact with every day.

Thank you for my job, Providing God.

LISTENING

Ask the Lord of the harvest, therefore, to send out workers into his harvest field.

LUKE 10:2

RETURNING

Bring to mind the grainfield again. You are the worker in the grainfield of your job, and the harvest is up to you.

Thanks
for This Day

CALMING
I will praise you, O LORD, with all my heart;
    I will tell of all your wonders.
I will be glad and rejoice in you;
    I will sing praise to your name,
O Most High.

PSALM 9:1-2

CENTERING
Cup your hands and imagine that you are holding a small seed in them. When you look at the seed, you have no idea what will come from it: whether it will be a beautiful blossom; a small, insignificant weed; or a giant tree. This seed symbolizes the possibilities that lie in this day.

Here is today, O God.

I don't know what this day will bring, although I like to think that I do. I have my schedule, my to-do list filled in, my agenda duly noted. I like to think that I have this day under my control.

But I know that's not how most days go.

I know that today I will be surprised by sorrows, joys, and challenges.

I know that today I will face both problems and adventures.

I know that today may be just an ordinary day, or it might be the most extraordinary day of my life.

And I know that you are the only one who knows what lies ahead. So I offer you this day.

(Raise your cupped hands and imagine giving the small seed to God.)

Here is today, O God. I give it to you, trusting that you will take whatever happens in this day and use it for your glory. I trust that whatever happens today, you will be with me.

Thank you for this day and for its endless possibilities. Thank you that I can face this day with you.

Here is today, O God:
a part of all the days we have spent together,
a part of all the days to come,
a part of who I am and where I am on
my journey,
a part of the plan that you have
for me.

Take this day. Use it to your glory. Thank you, God.

LISTENING

Though it is the smallest of all your seeds, yet when it grows, it is the largest of garden plants and becomes a tree, so that the birds of the air come and perch in its branches.

MATTHEW 13:32

RETURNING

Remind yourself that you have offered today to God. Remember lifting that small seed that represents today and giving it to God to be used as God sees fit.

Thanks
for Your Church

CALMING
I love the house where you live, O LORD,
    the place where your glory dwells.

PSALM 26:8

CENTERING
Imagine walking up the front steps of your church, opening the door, and entering. You are all alone, standing in the middle of the sanctuary. Look around at the furniture, the altar, and other familiar items in your place of worship.

PRAYING
Thank you, Providing God, for this building, this church, this house of worship.

Thank you for this place where I can meet with others to worship and glorify you.

Thank you for the peace and comfort I have found here.

Many other churches are around me.

Other sects,

    other beliefs,

        other rituals,

            other ways of worshiping you.

I wonder if this was part of your plan—that your people would break away from one another, divide among themselves, and create so many different churches with different congregations and so many different ideas of how to approach you.

Does what church I attend or how I worship you really matter? Does it matter how I approach you, how I pray, what my church looks like? I don't think so.

All that matters is that we come together as the body of Christ

to worship you,

    to praise you,

        to glorify your name,

            to acknowledge Jesus as our Savior.

Yet I thank you for my church. I thank you

for what it means to me, for what it has meant to my family, and for what it will mean to future generations. I thank you for the moments in this church when I have experienced your living presence.

I pray for all the members of my church, O God. May we all experience a new walk with you as we come together to worship you. Put in all our hearts a sense of the path that you have set for our congregation. Help us see your purpose clearly. Take away the barriers that stand between us and hinder us from being the people you want us to be.

Take away the jealousies,
    the angers,
        the arguments,
            the differences about doctrine,
                the beam in our own eyes.
Thank you for my church, Providing God.

LISTENING

And I tell you that you are Peter, and on this rock I will build my church, and the gates of Hades will not overcome it.

MATTHEW 16:18

Returning

Again think of yourself standing alone in the middle of your church sanctuary. Then slowly, one by one, begin filling the pews with people you know. Continue to fill the pews with visitors. Then fill the aisles and the back of the church, until your church is filled and overflowing with God's people.

Thanks
for Your Pastor

CALMING

You are my portion, O LORD;
    I have promised to obey your words.
I have sought your face with all my heart;
    be gracious to me according to your
        promise. . . .
Do good to your servant according to your
    word, O LORD.

PSALM 119:57-58, 65

CENTERING

Imagine your pastor working in a garden. See
him/her moving between the rows of plants,
hoeing, weeding, and digging. Take a moment
to fully realize that your pastor is a servant of
Jesus Christ.

PRAYING

I often wonder, dear Jesus, what life as one of your ordained ministers would be like. What would it be like to be more than just your follower—to be called as

a pastor,

a priest,

a minister,

a gardener who cares for your garden?

Here is *this person* you have called and the church has ordained.

I feel awe and amazement at my pastor's tender, loving, compassionate care for the people around *him/her*. Even when they show less than love and compassion in return, my pastor continues to love, care, shepherd, counsel, teach, guide, and minister to them.

I wonder how my pastor does it, Jesus. I wonder how *he/she* can keep going in the face of adversity: little progress in the people's spiritual growth; dissension in the congregation; bitterness, anger, and hard feelings in the people under *his/her* pastoral care. What's it like to try to bring your love into these circumstances?

Thank you so much, Jesus, for *this person*.

In *his/her* face, I see your face reflected.
In *his/her* kindness, I feel your
kindness.
In *his/her* words, I hear your
words.
In *his/her* ministry, I know
your love.

Thank you for my pastor. Today, at this very moment, pour your Holy Spirit upon *him/her*. Renew my pastor's faith, refresh *his/her* spirit, restore *his/her* energy, lift *him/her* up on the wings of eagles, and fill *him/her* with the certainty of your love and power.

Bless my pastor. Thank you, Lord Jesus.

LISTENING

I am the true vine, and my Father is the gardener.

JOHN 15:1

RETURNING

Return to the image of your pastor in the garden. See him or her as a gentle, loving gardener striving to cultivate healthy, beautiful plants in the garden God has given *him/her* to tend.

Thanks
for the Privilege of Prayer

CALMING
May my prayer be set before you like incense;
    may the lifting up of my hands be
       like the evening sacrifice.

PSALM 141:2

CENTERING
Imagine two things, one after another:
- smoke rising up into the air from a camp-
  fire on a still day,
- rain gently falling on your head.

PRAYING
Dear Son of God, it is so hard to imagine what
my life would be like without prayer.

Prayer is more than just a time of petition, of asking you for things. It is also a time of adoration, a time of praise, a time when I recognize all that you are to me:

Savior, Redeemer,
Shepherd,
Counselor, Teacher, and High Priest,
Morning Star and Lamb of God. . . .

Prayer is a time of forgiveness. As I recognize and confess the ways in which I have strayed from your path, I know that I am forgiven.

Prayer is so many things:

adoration, confession, thanksgiving,
forgiveness, supplication,
speaking, listening, begging,
laughing, crying, singing.

Prayer is more than just words. It is a connection with you.

Dear Jesus, when I pray, I am struck by the enormity of what I am doing. I am communicating with the Son of God! What an awesome thought that I can come to you; and, even more awesome, that you come to me; and, most awesome of all, that you answer my prayer.

Thank you, Jesus, that in my life I find innumerable quiet spaces where I can stop, say a few words to you, and know that we have connected in those few minutes.

I also thank you for those times when I can come together with my fellow Christians and pray. Together we lift you up in our midst. How I thank you for these experiences, Jesus. They are a blessing and a gift from you.

Listening

And whenever you pray, do not be like the hypocrites; for they love to stand and pray in the synagogues and at the street corners, so that they may be seen by others. Truly I tell you, they have received their reward. But whenever you pray, go into your room and shut the door and pray to your Father who is in secret; and your Father who sees in secret will reward you. When you are praying, do not heap up empty phrases as the Gentiles do; for they think that they will be heard because of their many words. Do not be like them, for your Father knows what you need before you ask him.

MATTHEW 6:5-8, NRSV

RETURNING

Think of your prayers as smoke rising up to heaven and of God's blessings as rain falling gently on your head. More comes down than goes up!

Thanks
for Your Body and Health

CALMING

Therefore my heart is glad and my tongue
rejoices;
my body also will rest secure,
because you will not abandon me to the grave,
nor will you let your Holy One see decay.

PSALM 16:9-10

CENTERING

Sit quietly, paying attention to the beating of
your heart. Hear the rhythm of your breathing.
Turn all your senses inward and become aware
of your body's rhythms, movements, and pulses.

PRAYING

Thank you, Creator God, for this life you gave
me. Thank you for breathing life into me.

You knew me even before I came to be; you knew me in my mother's womb.

Thank you for my health. Thank you that I can breathe, walk, see, hear. Thank you that I can talk and feel. Thank you for all these blessings you have given me.

As I sit here and listen to the rhythms of my body, I'm reminded that many people do not have all of these abilities. My few aches and pains are nothing compared to the suffering of so many people.

Dear God, keep me ever mindful of how blessed I am to have this body. So many times I am angry with my body:

I don't like its shape;

I don't like its weight;

I don't like certain parts of it;

I don't like what happens with it;

I complain, fret, fuss, and worry.

I forget to thank you. So now, O God, I thank you for this body and the health you have given me.

If my body should fail me, I trust you to take care of me. No matter what befalls me, no matter how I feel or what happens to my body, I know that you remain constant.

You are always there.
Thank you, God, for my body and health.

LISTENING

Therefore, if your whole body is full of light, and no part of it dark, it will be completely lighted, as when the light of a lamp shines on you.

LUKE 11:36

RETURNING

Continue to be aware of the movements and pulses of your body. Throughout the day continue to thank God that your body functions and allows you to live.

Thanks
for Your Country

CALMING

Blessed is the nation whose God is the LORD,
the people he chose for his inheritance.

PSALM 33:12

CENTERING

Think of a symbol of your country: the flag, the national anthem, a certain place, the pledge of allegiance, or a national leader. Whatever the symbol, focus your mind on it.

PRAYING

I thank you, O God, that I am a citizen of *this country.* I seldom think about how grateful I am to live here; perhaps only on national holidays do I think about that. Then I remember with other citizens what our country is, our roots and history. I listen to patriotic speeches, stand at attention, sing the national anthem, and feel proud to be a citizen of *this country*.

But as I listen to the news, read newspapers, and watch television, I realize how truly blessed I am to be a citizen of *this country*.

So many other countries in the world and their people suffer so greatly.

Wars, droughts, and famines.

Corruption, pain, and brutality.

Earthquakes, hurricanes, and floods.

Remind me often, O God, of how blessed I am. Remind me that despite what I may see around me in this country—crime, corruption, and disasters—these things are small compared to the daily sufferings many people experience.

We as a nation are so blessed.

Thank you for *this country*.

Thank you for my freedom to worship you.

Thank you that I can vote for my leaders.

Thank you that I can come and go as I choose within my country's borders.

Thank you that I can live my life as I wish.

Lord God, I ask you to be with our leaders. Give them wisdom, guide them, counsel them.

Give all the citizens of *this country* a strong sense of your presence, and help them to recognize their need for you.

Thank you for my country.

LISTENING
And this gospel of the kingdom will be preached in the whole world as a testimony to all nations, and then the end will come.

MATTHEW 24:14

RETURNING
Recall the symbol of your country. As you do so, imagine the cross of Jesus before it. How would Christ's leadership change your country?

Thanks
for Good Friday

CALMING

My God, my God, why have you forsaken me?
   Why are you so far from saving me,
      so far from the words of my groaning?
O my God, I cry out by day, but you do not
      answer,
   by night, and am not silent.

PSALM 22:1-2

CENTERING

Touch the palm of one hand with your other
hand, resting your fingers in the hollow.
Imagine what it would be like to have a nail
driven through that delicate part of your hand.
What would it be like to have your hand laid on
a rough piece of wood, to feel the first cold

prick of the nail, then the searing pain as it is driven into the wood through your hand? Sit quietly for a moment, continuing to touch the palm of your hand.

PRAYING

Dearest Jesus, Lamb of God, I can't imagine what it was like.

We talk so much about your death; there are
    so many stories,
        so many documentaries,
            so many movies,
                so many books,
                    so many sermons,
                        so many discussions . . .
so many ways we try to assess, to understand, to somehow come to grips with that horrible day.

And yet, dear Savior, I sit here touching my palm, trying to imagine what it would be like . . .

(Sit quietly for a moment.)

It's not that I can't imagine your pain. I just can't imagine the helplessness, desolation, and loneliness you must have felt at that moment.

I can't imagine why you didn't call on legions of angels to stop the whole horrible experience.

But you didn't. You *chose* to be the sacrifice.

I don't fully understand why you had to die or what happened when you offered yourself, but I do know that you endured all of this so that right now, right here, I could be praying to you.

Ransomed.

Redeemed.

Forgiven.

What a profound thought—

me, with all the things I am,

all the things I do,

and all the things I think—

me, a child of God. Forgiven. Loved.

Thank you, Jesus, for this day that we call Good Friday.

Thank you for all you endured and suffered for me. Thank you so much for doing what needed to be done so that at this moment, two thousand years later, I can say, "Thank you, Jesus, Savior, Lamb of God who takes away the sin of the world."

LISTENING

For even the Son of Man did not come to be served, but to serve, and to give his life as a ransom for many.

MARK 10:45

RETURNING

At every opportunity today, touch the palm of your hand and remember the sacrifice Jesus made for you.

Thanks
for Your Salvation

CALMING

I trust in your unfailing love;
    my heart rejoices in your salvation.

PSALM 13:5

CENTERING

Imagine a cross standing in a dark place. You can
see the vague outline of a figure on the cross.
Now light fills the area, illuminating the cross,
but no one is on the cross. Contemplate the
light-bathed empty cross for a few moments.

PRAYING

The cross is empty.

Dear Lord, you endured suffering and humili-
ation; you went through the agony of loneliness

and despair and left an empty cross.

Because you willingly died for the sins of the world, Christ Jesus, I am saved and redeemed, made right with God, forgiven and whole. Because you did that, I can call myself a Christian.

I can't imagine what my life would be like without you, Christ Jesus. Not just these moments that we spend together,

but every single waking,

breathing,

thinking

moment of my life.

You are so much a part of who I am, how I feel and think, how I believe, and what I do that to imagine not having you here is impossible.

I don't know how to thank you, dear Jesus, for this wonderful gift of my salvation. I can't begin to express how I feel when I realize what you did for me—not just for everyone else in the world, but for *me!*

How incredibly awesome the thought, that the Son of God would die for me.

Thank you, Jesus, for our walk together,

for the distance we've already come,

for the road that lies ahead.

Today I put myself into your hands. In doing

so, I acknowledge that you are my salvation and, because of an empty cross, I belong to you.

LISTENING

I give them eternal life, and they shall never perish; no one can snatch them out of my hand.

JOHN 10:28

RETURNING

Continue to think about the empty cross and its implications for your life.

Thanks
for Your Safety

CALMING
But let all who take refuge in you be glad;
  let them ever sing for joy.
Spread your protection over them,
  that those who love your name
  may rejoice in you.

PSALM 5:11-12

CENTERING
Imagine being held closely by someone who
cares for your safety and well-being. Feel yourself being held and rocked gently. Hear soft
whispers of assurance and the sound of a lullaby.

PRAYING

I was scared today, God, really scared. I thought I was in danger and my life was in jeopardy.

But I'm here now, talking with you. The danger has passed, and I am safe.

I didn't realize how scared I could be. And with that fear came a terrible anger.

I guess I thought that nothing bad could ever happen to me or my family.

I guess I believed that since I am a Christian, I would be protected from the sort of fear I experienced today.

I guess I thought that since you are always with me, I wouldn't experience the bad things of this world.

I was wrong. That's why I was so angry and scared. I wondered whether I would live, if this was the moment when I would finally see you face-to-face. And I was too involved in my fear to look forward to that moment.

Despite all this, Protecting God, you held me safe.

You were with me.

You carried me.

You sustained me.

You delivered me.

How I thank you for your loving, caring presence. Thank you for being with me at all times, even in times of danger and fear.

Thank you, my God.

LISTENING

Indeed, the very hairs of your head are all numbered. Don't be afraid; you are worth more than many sparrows.

LUKE 12:7

RETURNING

Sit quietly and experience the deep, warm, caring love of your gracious God as you imagine God holding you tightly and comforting you.

A QUIET

SPACE

to Pray for

Life's Stresses

When You
Have Too Much to Do

CALMING

Praise be to the Lord, to God our Savior,
   who daily bears our burdens.

PSALM 68:19

CENTERING

Remember how old movies indicated the passage of time? They'd show a calendar with rapidly turning pages, one after another, day after day, month after month. Imagine a calendar like this, but on each page is a to-do list. See page after page, list after list, things to do, everlasting things to do, and still more things to do. For a moment, watch this never-ending list flash rapidly through your mind.

Dear Jesus, I realize that my life is like that calendar of pages with list after list of things to do. Every morning in my waking moment, my first thought isn't of you but of all the things I must do this day.

Even before I get out of bed, I don't think about you; I don't think about me; I don't think about anything but that list of things to do before the day is over.

No wonder I awaken with my mind racing and my heart pounding!

And when the day is over, is my last thought of you, dear Savior? No, because I worry about all the things I didn't get done today, and I'm already thinking about all the things I have to do tomorrow.

I want to stop. I want to rid my brain of the everlasting to-do lists. I want to get off the treadmill of each day.

This is not the path you intended for me, having every hour of every day filled with things that must be done:

things I want to do,

things I don't want to do,

things other people expect me to do,

> things I know I must do,
>> things given to me to do,
>>> always things to do. . . .

I want to stop! I want to take a deep breath and let all these things go. I want to feel the freedom of having a day ahead of me in which there is enough time and enough space to let you in.

Dear Jesus, during this day help me quiet all the thoughts that fill my head—where I must go, who I must see, and what I must do. In their place, give me a sense of your order, your peace, and your time.

Help me to understand that you are in control, and I can trust you with my day. Help me to realize that nothing on my to-do list is important if it is not what you want me to do.

I give all my tasks to you and trust you to bring order to them. In these moments, dear Jesus, come to me, be with me, and free me from the tyranny of "to do."

LISTENING

Come to me, all you who are weary and burdened, and I will give you rest. Take my yoke upon you and learn from me, for I am gentle and humble in heart, and you will find rest for your souls. For my yoke is easy and my burden is light.

MATTHEW 11:28-30

RETURNING

Return to the image of the calendar with rapidly flashing pages of to-do lists. Imagine that the calendar pages stop turning and the to-do list on the top page slowly disappears until only a blank page remains. This is today.

Imagine that you and Jesus together decide what must be done today: how to do it, when to do it, or whether to do it at all. As you go through the day, if you feel pressured because you have too much to do, remember the image of the blank page on top of the calendar. Let it remind you that Jesus can help you sort through the day.

When There's No Time for You and Your Needs

CALMING

But I trust in you, O LORD;
　I say, "You are my God."
My times are in your hands.

PSALM 31:14-15

CENTERING

Imagine a huge clock with rapidly moving hands. The hour hand races from hour to hour, the minute hand spins wildly, and the second hand is just a blur. Watch the moving clock hands for a moment; then imagine them suddenly becoming still.

Trustworthy God, that racing clock is the way my days look to me. Time races by with no time left for anything I want to do. There always seems to be enough time for everyone else, for the things others expect me to do. There even seems to be time for things I don't want to do. But there's never time for me.

Am I not important? Isn't there any time in this twenty-four-hour day that I can call mine? Surely there must be a minute or two that I can have just for me.

A minute or two? That's what it boils down to, doesn't it? A minute or two for me.

O God, I'm tired of continually trying to squeeze out just a few minutes for myself. I resent everyone else's controlling my time, and I become angry when others expect more of my time. I need time too!

I know that you care for me. You even know the number of hairs on my head!

I know that you hold me in your hand.

I know that you are the Creator of the universe and that time is in your hands.

If I know all these things, Lord, why can't I believe that you can find time to give to me?

All I can do is trust that somehow, somewhere in this day, you will give me the gift of time: time just for me and no one else. I pray that in that small space of time, I will find you.

LISTENING

All that belongs to the Father is mine. That is why I said the Spirit will take from what is mine and make it known to you.

JOHN 16:15

RETURNING

Let the image of the stopped clock remind you that at any moment God can give you the gift of time—if you ask for it. Throughout the day, focus on the stopped clock and look for the gift of time that awaits you.

When You're Waiting for Someone Who's Late

CALMING

Wait for the LORD;
  be strong and take heart
  and wait for the LORD.

PSALM 27:14

CENTERING

Sit still, consciously stopping all movement in your body. If there is noise or movement around you, tune it out as best you can. If you are in a place where you can do so, close your eyes and concentrate on the rhythm of your breathing. (Breathe deeply and slowly.)

Praying

I'm waiting for *this person*, O God, and getting anxious about *him/her*. I'm also angry because I resent spending this time waiting.

I want to do something useful with this time, but my anger and anxiety get in the way. I keep wondering where *this person* is and why *he/she* hasn't called. My anger and anxiety are growing.

This person must not care about me and my time. If *he/she* did, I wouldn't be sitting here now. It's not the first time I've waited for *this person*. It's as if

his/her time is more important than mine,

his/her needs are more important,

his/her feelings are more important.

So I'm left here . . . waiting.

I'm not good at waiting. I worry that something has happened to *this person*. Has *he/she* been in an accident? I imagine all kinds of horrible scenarios. Then I get angry. That's the hardest of all.

I imagine that *he/she* forgot our appointment,

that *he/she* got caught up in something

more interesting than being with me,

that *he/she* doesn't care about what I

feel or think.

So I'm sitting here, waiting. Doing nothing.

O God, I just realized what I could be doing right now. Instead of worrying and feeling angry about *this person,* I could be praying for *him/her!* What a wonderful heaven-sent opportunity: a special gift of time you have given me. Not time to be waiting, worrying, and fretting, but time to be praying for *this person.*

So I lift up *this person* to you. I see *him/her* with an inward eye of concern.

I ask you to bless *him/her,*
> to touch *him/her,*
>> to be with *him/her* in a tangible way
>>> in this time while I sit here
>>>> waiting, waiting, waiting . . .
>>>>> and praying.

LISTENING

The right time for me has not yet come; for you any time is right.

JOHN 7:6

RETURNING

Whenever you must wait for someone or some event, take time to pray especially for the person or happening. View the waiting time as a God-given opportunity to create a space in which you can sit quietly and lay your petitions at the throne of grace.

When You're
Worried about Money

CALMING
I will bless her with abundant provisions;
   her poor will I satisfy with food.

PSALM 132:15

CENTERING
Take a moment to think of all the areas where
you have money concerns. As each thought
comes into your mind, imagine writing the concern on a piece of paper. See yourself placing
each piece of paper in Jesus' open hands.

PRAYING
Here they are, Jesus—all the things I'm worried
about. Debts, payments, bills, accounts . . .

   I feel guilty for having so many money worries in my life. I feel like I've let you down by worrying about something so worldly. I know that there are others who hurt more than I do:

They struggle against greater bonds than I do,
        they dwell in a poverty I can't even begin
            to comprehend.

                I know these things, and yet . . .

I have bills to pay and not enough money to pay them. That's the bottom line of my worries. All the righteous platitudes in the world can't change that fact.

That's why I feel such despair. Thoughts of money—how much I have, how much I need, how much I want—keep surfacing in my mind. I can't seem to get away from them.

These thoughts consume me,
    blotting out all other thoughts—
        for others around me,
            for you.

It shouldn't be this way. I feel like I'm being crushed by the burden of my money thoughts.

I ask for freedom right now, dear Jesus.

Release me today. I give these worries to you, placing them into your precious nail-scarred hands. I trust you to take them from me. In their place, please give me the freedom that comes from knowing that you care and watch over me. Remind me often that you know my needs and that you will provide for them.

LISTENING

Consider how the lilies grow. They do not labor or spin. Yet I tell you, not even Solomon in all his splendor was dressed like one of these. If that is how God clothes the grass of the field, which is here today, and tomorrow is thrown into the fire, how much more will he clothe you, O you of little faith!

LUKE 12:27-28

RETURNING

Reflect on the truth of Jesus' words and feel the freedom they give you. Throughout the day as a money worry comes to mind, visualize the worry written on a piece of paper, and mentally place that paper in Jesus' hands. Continually give the worries to him, even if you have to do so ten or twenty times. Each time thank Jesus for the freedom from worry that he promised.

When You
Feel Disorganized

CALMING

I was pushed back and about to fall,
> but the LORD helped me.
The LORD is my strength and my song;
> he has become my salvation.

CENTERING

Imagine that you're in the same place where you are now, but every inch of that room is cluttered and jumbled with stuff. Imagine that bags overflow in every corner; piles of papers cover every available space; boxes spill their contents onto the floor. See this overcrowded, messy room in your mind's eye.

Now imagine a gentle, warm breeze blowing

softly through the room. As it blows, items begin to put themselves into order. Drawers close, boxes disappear, papers reshuffle, and the room becomes a quiet, orderly space.

Praying

My life feels so disorganized, Holy Spirit. It seems as if everything around me is piling up. It's not just the drawers that need reorganizing, the kitchen that needs cleaning, or the heap of stuff in the garage that needs sorting—it's everything:

>my daily schedule crammed full of tasks,
>>my house crying out for a major cleaning,
>>>my office with the overflowing
>>>in box and stacks of junk—

even my relationships are disorganized.

I feel disjointed, out of control, out of touch.

Bring order into my life. Help me sort through all the things around me.

Help me see what needs to be kept,
>what needs to be thrown away,
>>and what needs to be changed.

Help me organize my life by putting things where they need to be, removing them from places where they shouldn't be, and changing things that shouldn't be.

O Holy Spirit, even as I say this, I feel fear. I know that things need to change. I know, deep in my heart, that my life's disorganization is symptomatic of a deeper disorganization.

I need your gentle breeze to blow through my spiritual life. I need your strong wind to sort through the stacks of issues I don't want to face. I need your quiet presence as I deal with the unspoken prayers, the unfulfilled desires, the unrecognized emotions I have hidden away.

Holy Spirit, come now, in this moment, and in the recesses of my heart, begin the process of organization. Begin to sweep out the dark corners, sift through the crammed closets, and blow through all my dark places. May you blow through my life every day. Through your power, bring order into all the chaos around me.

LISTENING

Martha, Martha, . . . you are worried and upset about many things, but only one thing is needed. Mary has chosen what is better, and it will not be taken away from her.

LUKE 10:41-42

Returning

Throughout the day as you come across symptoms of your disorganization, close your eyes and imagine the wind of the Holy Spirit blowing across it. As the wind blows, you gain clarity about dealing with the disorganization.

When You're Procrastinating

CALMING

But now, Lord, what do I look for?
    My hope is in you.
Save me from all my transgressions;
    do not make me the scorn of fools.

PSALM 39:7-8

CENTERING

Imagine walking in water as you attempt to cross a shallow, flowing stream. Suddenly the water becomes thick and muddy. Where the water was once clear and sparkling, it is now dark and turgid. The water becomes muddier and muddier until it turns into a thick quagmire. You are unable to move.

That's me, Lord Jesus—stuck in the middle of the stream. I know I have things to do, places to go, and people I should call or write or visit.

Yet, I'm stuck in the middle of the stream.

It's as if I am in thick mud. I can't seem to make myself do what I need to do. I keep putting things off. I keep hoping that tomorrow I'll feel like doing them.

And when tomorrow comes, nothing has changed. I'm still stuck in the mud, still in the middle of the stream, still hoping to feel better tomorrow. I simply can't get going. I look at everything I'm putting off, and I feel an overwhelming sense of guilt.

I'm still stuck in the middle of the stream.

I don't know why I procrastinate. I don't know what causes me to be unable to make a decision, move ahead, or do what needs to be done. I don't know if the cause is fear, laziness, anger, fatigue, or boredom.

I just know that I'm stuck in the middle of this stream.

Christ Jesus, I need you to help me move on. I need your help to move out of this mud of indecision and procrastination.

I can't do this alone.

Help me make that leap of faith. Help me not to look down at the mud around my feet but to you in front of me, beckoning me on.

Remove me from the middle of the stream, Christ Jesus.

LISTENING

Therefore everyone who hears these words of mine and puts them into practice is like a wise man who built his house on the rock. The rain came down, the streams rose, and the winds blew and beat against that house; yet it did not fall, because it had its foundation on the rock.

MATTHEW 7:24-25

RETURNING

When you find yourself procrastinating, close your eyes and imagine your feet sticking in the thick mud of indecision or dread. Then see the quagmire dissolve into clear, sparkling water. Walk through it to the shore on the other side and begin the task you need to do.

When You
Feel Overwhelmed

CALMING

He reached down from on high
  and took hold of me;
he drew me out of deep waters.

PSALM 18:16

CENTERING

Imagine that you are in a boat, rocking wildly on the choppy waves of a rough ocean. Then the waves become calm swells; the boat moves gently with the water. Feel the rhythm as the boat lifts and falls like a cradle being rocked. Allow yourself to relax.

PRAYING

Ever-present God, thank you for being here with me right now. In the chaos of my life, I often forget that you are always with me, always seeking to bring me peace.

There are so many things in my life:
demands of others,
needs of others,
expectations of others—
always "others."

I have so much to do,
so many responsibilities on my shoulders.

I feel overwhelmed, as if the world around me is a heaving, crashing sea; and I am adrift in a small boat, unable to keep the waves from closing over me.

Only you can bring order out of this chaos. Say the word, All-Powerful God, and I know that the seas will be calmed, and I will be safe. I know this—yet I'm afraid to let go of the tiller and trust you.

My mind skitters around my many concerns:
What if something doesn't get done?
What if someone is angry with my
actions?
What if . . . ?

Even as I say these words, I can hear how foolish they are. You, the God of my life, are also the God of order. Bring order to my life, and in doing so, take care of all those concerns that rise up around me like storm waves. Calm the seas of my busyness; still the waters of my "doingness." Let me drift on the gentle swells of your love and care.

As you did for Peter, give me the courage to step boldly out onto the waters around me, knowing that you will never let me sink beneath them. Here, in this Quiet Space, I stretch out my hand to you, feeling the power of your touch, the strength of your will.

Thank you, O God, that the same hand that stilled the waters holds my hand.

LISTENING

I have told you these things, so that in me you may have peace. In this world you will have trouble. But take heart! I have overcome the world.

JOHN 16:33

RETURNING

Throughout the day, imagine yourself on a calm ocean, quietly rocking in a small boat.

When You
Want Time to Pass Quickly

CALMING

The LORD reigns, he is robed in majesty;
    the LORD is robed in majesty
    and is armed with strength.
The world is firmly established;
    it cannot be moved.

PSALM 93:1

CENTERING

Imagine that you're on a train traveling slowly through the countryside. You're enjoying the view from a window. Then the train begins to speed up; faster and faster it goes until the scenery outside becomes a blur. You no longer see where you've been, where you are, or where you're going. All you see is the blur outside.

Praying

O God, I seem to spend my whole life wanting to rush ahead. I'm always thinking of tomorrow, next week, next month, next year. I'm always wishing time would hurry by.

I'm seldom here,
> right here,
>> in this moment,
>>> at this time,
>>>> being part of what is around me.

My mind is always elsewhere—anywhere but here. I keep wishing the clock would race ahead so that I can get to whatever I want most, that I can enjoy whatever I'm looking forward to, that I can go wherever I want to go.

I'm not here.

I miss so much of my life by not living in the present:
> so many things I don't see around me,
>> so many people I never touch,
>>> so many moments I miss now because
>>>> they're not part of my future.

Instead I watch the clock and wish the time would rush by. I watch the clock and wish away my life.

I'm never here.

Perhaps that's why I sometimes find it hard to connect with you, O God, because connecting with you is a here-and-now thing; and I'm never now—I'm always in the future.

Help me to be here in the present. Help me to enjoy this very moment, this very second, this very millisecond.

Remind me that the abundant life you offer is now. Remind me that tomorrow will take care of itself and that today is all I have.

Let me enjoy my journey today. Wash away from my mind all thoughts about what I'd rather be doing or where I'd rather be at this moment. Take away the urge to push time forward. Help me to sit back and to simply *be*.

LISTENING
No one knows about that day or hour, not even the angels in heaven, nor the Son, but only the Father.

MATTHEW 24:36

RETURNING
Imagine the train slowing down so that the scenery outside the windows becomes clear. So much is available for you to look at and enjoy.

Throughout the day as you feel yourself rushing and wishing that time would hurry by, go back to the train, sit still, and enjoy the view from the window.

When You're Anxious

When anxiety was great within me,
   your consolation brought joy to my soul.

PSALM 94:19

CENTERING

Imagine a still pool of dark water. A pebble drops into the middle of the pool. Ripples begin to spread, moving toward the outer edges of the pool. Another pebble drops. More ripples. Another pebble. More ripples. Eventually the pool is covered with ripples bouncing into one another, back and forth, up and down, side to side, edge to edge.

I'd like for my life to be like that still pool, O God, but I fear it's more like the one with all the ripples. All my thoughts about *this situation* are like stones dropping into the stillness of my life. The ripples spread from one part of my life to another until every moment is consumed by thoughts, concerns, worries about *this situation*. I can think of nothing else, just *this situation*, and my life is full of disturbing ripples.

And I can't focus on you.

All-Powerful God, I want to be rid of all the ripples of concern and worry. The only way I can do that is to stop the stones of thought from falling into my pool. And God, I don't know how to do that.

I need your help.

Help me see how destructive worry is.

Help me look into the pool and see the disturbances that all these thoughts cause.

Help me realize that you are the only one who can take care of my anxiety.

Help me see that all my anxious thoughts won't make one bit of difference in *this situation*.

Help me put away these thoughts.

O God, right now, I turn my eyes back to

you. In this moment, I put away my thoughts of *this situation* and concentrate on you, only you: my God.

Right now, I trust that you are working in me and in my thoughts. I trust that you will help me throughout today and the coming days to put aside the thoughts of *this situation,* and in their place, to think only of you and your loving care for me. Thank you, God, for returning calm and peace to the pool of my life.

LISTENING

And can any of you by worrying add a single hour to your span of life? If then you are not able to do so small a thing as that, why do you worry about the rest?

LUKE 12:25-26, NRSV

RETURNING

Throughout the day, as your thoughts return to your situation, close your eyes briefly and imagine the pool covered in ripples. Imagine those ripples slowly smoothing out and disappearing until the pool becomes peaceful and still.

When You're Running Late

CALMING

Answer me, O LORD,
  out of the goodness of your love;
in your great mercy turn to me.

PSALM 69:16

CENTERING

Picture yourself walking slowly and comfortably on a treadmill in a large, empty room. Then the treadmill begins to speed up. You're finding it difficult to keep up the pace. You start running. The treadmill speeds up more, and you run a little faster. The treadmill speeds up even more. You're beginning to feel desperate because you can't keep up anymore.

PRAYING

Lord Jesus, why do I always feel that I'm racing against the clock? Why is every moment of my day a race against time?

Why am I always running out of time?

Why am I always running late?

Why am I so tired?

I simply have too much to do. It doesn't matter how much I plan. I do all the right things. I lay out my day, prioritize tasks, include my appointments, and leave time for the unexpected.

And still, I'm always running late.

Somewhere, somehow this craziness has to stop. But how? I feel powerless. I don't know what to do. I just know that I don't like living this way. And right now, Lord Jesus, I'm running late. Again.

Jesus, I give up! I give up trying to take control of my time, trying to bring some order into my schedule. I lift up my concerns to you. My plans, my commitments, my appointments, my schedules, my lists—they're all yours.

And most of all, I give you this moment when I'm running late.

Dear Jesus, take my daily schedule. Put your hand upon it and bring order to it. I trust you to take care of the time that I have. I trust you to help me go where I need to go, do what I need to do—all with a sense of time that only you can give me. Lord Jesus, it's all yours. I'm going to stop running. Thank you, Jesus.

LISTENING

If you hold to my teaching, you are really my disciples. Then you will know the truth, and the truth will set you free.

JOHN 8:31-32

RETURNING

Whenever you begin to feel rushed, hurried, or late, imagine yourself on the treadmill, slowing down until you can walk comfortably. Be assured that Jesus has your time in his hands.

A QUIET
SPACE
to Pray for
a Relationship

&

Your Relationship
with Your Life Partner

CALMING

We wait in hope for the LORD;
  he is our help and our shield.
In him our hearts rejoice,
  for we trust in his holy name.
May your unfailing love rest upon us, O LORD,
  even as we put our hope in you.

PSALM 33:20-22

CENTERING

Sit quietly, letting your mind fill with images of your partner. Picture this person in various circumstances: with friends, alone with you, with your family. Choose an image that makes you feel happy. Enjoy reliving the feelings of that time.

Here is *this person,* O God.

When I was a little girl, I thought I knew who my life partner would be: a Prince Charming or a knight in shining armor. I didn't expect to find someone like *this person.* Thank you for bringing *this person* into my life.

Thank you for the wonderful times we've had together. Thank you for the tears and the laughter, the sorrow and the joy, and the love that is always between us.

Thank you for the life we've built together.

Thank you for all we do together.

Thank you for what we are together.

I pray, God, that you will put yourself in our relationship and become a part of who we are. Create a strong bond between us, so that we become a threefold cord that is not quickly broken.

Create a cord so strong that together—you, *this person,* and I—we will be able to withstand everything that lies ahead of us.

Create a cord so gentle that it will be a source of joy for us as we continue life's journey.

Create an enduring cord that will always bind us to you, so that no power on earth can destroy it.

Thank you, God, for *this person* and the relationship you have given us.

Listening

For this reason a man will leave his father and mother and be united to his wife, and the two will become one flesh.

MATTHEW 19:5

Returning

Imagine a large, thick cord made of three strands twisted together. This strong cord binds you and your partner to each other and to God. Remember this image at times when you feel unhappy, angry, disappointed, or worried about your relationship with your partner.

Your Relationship
with Your Son

CALMING

Our steps are made firm by the LORD,
  when he delights in our way;
though we stumble, we shall not fall headlong,
  for the LORD holds us by the hand.

PSALM 37:23-24, NRSV

CENTERING

Bring to mind an image of your son, one of a time when both of you were happy. It doesn't need to be current. You can remember your son as a baby, a toddler, a preschooler, a school-age child, or a young man. Concentrate on this image for a few moments, reliving the feeling of happiness.

PRAYING

Here is my son, Gracious God.

I thank you for him.

Thank you for letting me be part of his life.

Thank you for the joy he has brought me and for the challenges he has given me.

Thank you for my son.

I look at him and see the man that he will become or is, and I rejoice, O God, for his life.

I thank you, that you have chosen me to be his mother. Sometimes he and I don't see eye to eye, but I love my son. Whether now is a rough time or a good time in our relationship, it's a time you have given to us.

Gracious God, I ask you to stand between me and my son. In that way everything I say, everything I do, everything I think will be filtered through you before it reaches him. You'll surround all my thoughts and actions with your love before they reach my son.

Be an intermediary between us,
a pathway of love joining us,
a part of our bond,
a channel of all our thoughts
and feelings about each
other.

Regardless of our current relationship, I ask you to strengthen the bond between my son and me. If the bond is weak and broken, help me find ways to repair it. If the bond is strong and sure, I ask you to reinforce it.

Help me, O God, to continue in my own way, to the best of my abilities, to mentor my son, to guide him, and to be a warm, safe haven for him when he is distressed.

Steadfast God, put your hand upon my son. Guard him and keep him.

Guide him on life's path. Lead him gently but surely toward you. Keep him safe and secure.

Thank you, O God, for the gift of my son. Thank you for the laughter, the tears, the joy, and the sorrow. Thank you for all he has brought to my life and all he means to me.

LISTENING

Is there anyone among you who, if your child asks for bread, will give a stone? Or if the child asks for a fish, will give a snake? If you then, who are evil, know how to give good gifts to your children, how much more will your Father in heaven give good things to those who ask him!

MATTHEW 7:9-11, NRSV

RETURNING

When thoughts of your son come to mind, recall the image of him at a time when you felt the happiest with him. Hold that image close to you, reminding yourself of that moment in time with him. Enjoy reliving that feeling today, and remind yourself that your love for each other is still present.

Your Relationship
with Your Daughter

CALMING

Delight yourself in the LORD
    and he will give you the desires of your heart.

PSALM 37:4

CENTERING

Bring to mind an image of your daughter, one of a time when the two of you were happy. It may be a current image or one of her as a child. Hold this image in your mind. Enjoy reliving the good feelings, and sit quietly for a moment.

PRAYING

Here is my daughter, O God.
    I thank you for her.

Thank you for allowing me to be part of her life and her to be part of mine.

Thank you for the good times we have had and for the times of sorrow as well.

Here is my daughter, O God.

She is part of my life, part of who I am, and part of who I will become. We are inextricably woven together. I see in her many of my own qualities. I see in her my own doubts and fears. I see in her my own joys and excitements.

My heart's desire is that she will have all the joy that life can bring. And in those times when joy seems far away, Loving God, be with her.

O God, I ask you to stand between my daughter and me.

Between us so that whatever happens must pass through you.

Between us so that all that is said is filtered through your loving care and concern.

Between us so that my words, thoughts, and actions are transformed by your love into love for my daughter.

Remind me often that I was once like her. I may not see it now, but in her reside the seeds of what I once was.

Remind me often that I may not always like what she does or approve of what she has done, but she is my daughter, a gift from you.

I ask today that you hold her close in the palm of your hand. Guard her, guide her, and keep her. Thank you, O God.

LISTENING
Whoever welcomes one of these little children in my name welcomes me; and whoever welcomes me does not welcome me but the one who sent me.

MARK 9:37

RETURNING
Throughout the day recall the happy image of your daughter. Whenever you have negative thoughts about her, bring that image to mind and relive the moment in time when the two of you were happy together. Remind yourself often that your love for each other is still there.

Your Relationship
with Your Mother

CALMING

We will not hide them from their children;
   we will tell the next generation
the praiseworthy deeds of the LORD,
   his power, and the wonders he has done.

PSALM 78:4

CENTERING

Take a moment to allow images of your mother
to flow through your mind. See her as you remember her at different stages of your life.
Think of her at times when she was smiling,
laughing, frowning, and angry. Try to see her as
a whole person.

Here is my mother, O God.

The mother-daughter relationship is complex. A special bond exists between mothers and daughters—a bond that can be a joy or a burden, that can bring both tears and laughter.

So much of my life is tied up with my mother in one way or another. It's hard for me to be my own person when I'm with my mother. In her eyes, I am still a little girl. We must work at our new relationship: the relationship of an adult to an adult.

Here is my mother, O God.

Help me to understand that she wants only the best for me, even if at times this doesn't seem true.

Be with me when I am with my mother. Stand between us. Act as a buffer for all of the thoughts and memories, ideas and imaginings, events and occasions that are always present when we are together—these bring so much baggage to our relationship.

O God, I'd like to have a relationship with my mother that is based solely upon our love for each other. This can only happen with your help. As you stand between the two of us, take our thoughts and actions, filter them through your love, and increase our love for each other.

Here is my mother, O God.

How I thank you for this special bond, this unique relationship you have given me. I thank you so much for allowing me to be a part of my mother's life and her to be part of mine.

I pray that you will give each of us the best of the other person.

LISTENING

Here is your mother.

JOHN 19:27

RETURNING

Continue to sit quietly and think about your mother. Try to view her as a child of God. Bring her face to your mind, an image that makes you feel good about her, hold it there, and enjoy it.

Your Relationship
with Your Father

CALMING

But from everlasting to everlasting
    the LORD's love is with those who fear him,
and his righteousness with their
    children's children.

PSALM 103:17

CENTERING

Bring to mind an image of your father. Choose an image in which you feel happy and relaxed, one that brings back good memories. Hold this image in your mind for a few moments and enjoy the feelings it recalls.

PRAYING

Here is my father, O God.

I thank you for him.

Thank you for making him part of my life and me part of his.

Thank you for the guidance he has given me.

Thank you for his good example.

Thank you for everything he has done for me.

Here is my father, O God.

So many other people never know what it is to have a kind and loving father. So many other people don't know their father, or they have a father who doesn't care for them.

As I grow older, O God, I appreciate my father more and more. I begin to realize how many ways he has shaped my life. I also realize how wise he is, how patient and loving.

Forgive me for the times I've criticized him,

The times I have burdened him with my
problems,

The times I have grieved him with my
behavior.

Like you, heavenly Father, he has always forgiven me, loved me, and held me tight in his warm embrace.

Thank you for my father, O God. Thank you for all he means to me. I thank you for the feelings we have for each other—in the past, now, and in the future. Bless our relationship.

Hold us both in the palm of your hand. Be with us when we are together:

Be in our words to each other,

be in our thoughts about each other,

be in our trust in each other,

and be in our love for each other.

Bless my father, O God. Put your loving hand upon him and give him peace and joy. In these moments, let him feel your presence in his life, and let him know that he is loved.

Listening

But while he was still a long way off, his father saw him and was filled with compassion for him; he ran to his son, threw his arms around him and kissed him.

LUKE 15:20

Returning

Continue to think about the image of your father, one that makes you feel good. Hold this image close to you, enjoy those feelings, and then slowly let the image float away as you begin to return to your everyday life.

Your Relationship with Your Grandparent

&

CALMING

Teach me your way, O LORD,
    and I will walk in your truth;
give me an undivided heart,
    that I may fear your name.

PSALM 86:11

CENTERING

Bring to mind the face of *your grandparent*. See *him/her* as clearly as you can. Notice all the signs of aging that may be in *his/her* face. Let your mind dwell on *his/her* face for a moment and appreciate these signs of a life lived.

O God, I thank you for *this person.* All the wisdom, all the knowledge, all the experiences that *he/she* has are mine as well. Like a flower that blooms and then produces seed to scatter upon the ground around it, *this person* scatters seeds upon me.

I feel those seeds taking root,
> growing deep within me,
>> changing who and what I am.

They bloom into knowledge,
> into wisdom,
>> into experience,
>>> into all the things that *this person* is.

And now they are a part of me.

Eternal God, as I look at *this person,* I realize that growing old is not frightening. I realize that growing old is part of life and that this process brings us to a point where we are able to spread the seeds of who we are to those we love.

I thank you, O God, for the openness and willingness of *this person* to share with me so that *he/she* will become part of me. In *him/her,* I see an example of what I want to be like. I want to grow old in a way that allows me to share with others around me. In the richness of age, I want to share so many things that you have given me:

all that I am,

all that I know,

and all that I have.

I thank you for *this person.*

I thank you for *his/her* impact on my life.

I thank you for the laughter we share, the love we have for each other, the joy we take in each other's company.

Yet, as I think about *this person* and bring *his/her* face to my mind, I feel a pang of sorrow, for in the deepening lines, the graying hair, the tremor of the head, and the softening of the voice, I see signs of an ending.

When that ending comes, Eternal God, I pray that you'll take *him/her* home to you, hold *him/her* close, and thank *him/her* for all that *he/she* has done for me. Thank you for *this person.*

LISTENING

Return home and tell how much God has done for you.

LUKE 8:39

RETURNING

Think about your grandparent again and imagine a beautiful flower bursting into a wonderful blossom. The blossom fades, seeds form, and a gentle breeze scatters the seeds into the wind. Thank God that some of the seeds of love from this person are planted in your heart.

Your Relationship with a Difficult Boss

CALMING

LORD, you have assigned me my portion
   and my cup;
you have made my lot secure.

PSALM 16:5

CENTERING

Imagine a cup in the middle of a table. The cup slowly fills with liquid until the liquid spills over the sides and flows across the table. In your imagination, see the liquid continuing to pour out of the cup in an ever-widening pool.

PRAYING

Dear Jesus, you are the Lord of my life. Yet in my daily life, I serve someone else—not with the love and devotion I give you but with the uncomfortable bonds of necessity. I know that you have my life in your hand, and that includes my job, but I have difficulty accepting that my boss is part of your plan for me.

This person has so much power in my life. *He/she* is in my thoughts as I wake up and as I go to sleep.

His/her words haunt me.

His/her actions anger me.

His/her presence threatens me.

I can't get away from *him/her*. Every day, every day . . . I must face *him/her*.

I know that you want me to turn the other cheek, to love my enemies, to pray for those who are cruel to me. I know all the ways I should act, dear Jesus.

But when I try to do these things, it's as if a heavy cloud of anger and despair were blocking my actions. I feel powerless against it.

Surely my boss is part of your purpose for my life. Help me to believe this.

Jesus, please free me from thoughts of cynicism and doubt. Help me to see that what I do can have a profoundly positive effect on *this person's* life.

Give me the inner strength I need to move beyond my feelings for *him/her*. Help me see that I can be your instrument to reach *him/her*. Open my heart to the possibilities in this situation.

LISTENING

Pay attention to what you hear; the measure you give will be the measure you get, and still more will be given you. For to those who have, more will be given; and from those who have nothing, even what they have will be taken away.

MARK 4:24-25, NRSV

RETURNING

Your task is to be an overflowing source of God's love to your boss. Close your eyes and imagine the cup on the table again. That cup is you, and the liquid is the love of Jesus. The table is your boss. Throughout the day, whenever you feel angry, threatened, or overwhelmed by your boss, imagine the cup. Fill it in your mind and let it overflow.

Your Relationship
with a Friend

Calming

For the sake of my relatives and friends,
I will say, "Peace be within you."

Psalm 122:8, nrsv

Centering

Think about your friend. See this person clearly.
Bring to mind a happy time the two of you
shared. Enjoy reliving that moment.

Praying

Here is my friend, O God. Thank you for *this
person.* Thank you for all we share together.

Thank you for the bond of love between us.

Thank you for our trust in each other.

Thank you for our friendship.

He/she has enriched my life. So many times, I have trusted my friend to take my concerns, to listen to my worries, to hear my joys and my sorrows. And I have done the same for *him/her*.

Gracious God, I pray that you will reach out your hand and bless *this person*.

Touch *this person* with your lovingkindness. Fill *his/her* heart with your light, joy, and peace.

Wrap your love around *him/her*.

Let *him/her* know that *he/she* is truly loved, not just by me but also by you.

As I pray for my friend, I realize that my closeness with *him/her* is just a shadow compared to the closeness I have with you.

You are always there,
always waiting,
always ready,
always willing,
always available.

Help me to be the same kind of friend to *this person*. Help me to be waiting, ready, willing, and available. Open my ears so that I can listen with your loving attention; give me the words to speak so that *he/she* can hear your words of love; keep me in your perfect will so that all I say and do with my friend reflects you.

LISTENING

You are my friends if you do what I command you. I do not call you servants any longer, because the servant does not know what the master is doing; but I have called you friends, because I have made known to you everything that I have heard from the Father.

JOHN 15:14-15, NRSV

RETURNING

As you think about your friend, continue to think about the friendship you have with Jesus, and realize that your friendship with Jesus is a model for your friendship with this person.

Your Relationship
with Your Prayer Group

CALMING
The trees of the LORD are well watered,
the cedars of Lebanon that he planted.
There the birds make their nests;
the stork has its home in the pine trees.

PSALM 104:16-17

CENTERING
Imagine a wide grassy field. In the middle of the field stands a single tree. Think about how the tree looks standing alone in this expanse.

PRAYING
Dear God, I am like that single tree standing in the middle of the field. Sometimes I feel so alone in my Christian walk.

I am only one person—a voice crying in the wilderness. Yet, when I'm with this prayer group, I am part of a much larger whole. When we come together, we are no longer solitary persons but the body of Christ.

How wonderful it is when we gather together and talk about how we have experienced you. How uplifting it is when we relate how you come into our lives. How awesome it is to be part of your power working through and in us.

But sometimes, Lord, we get offtrack.

We complain,

we get angry with one another,

we fuss about small things,

we take sides on unimportant issues.

We forget that our purpose is to be the body of Christ.

We forget that you are there with us as we come together.

Loving God, I pray that we will feel your presence as we meet. Continue to remind us that the reason we meet together is to glorify you, to lift you up before all people, to continually praise you for all you have done.

Help us remember that together we can pray

for others. Turn our eyes from inward looking to outward looking. Show us the need around us, and give us wisdom to know how to pray for that need.

Thank you, O God, for bringing us together.

Thank you for encouraging each of us to be part of *this group.*

Thank you, God, that you have given each of us particular gifts and talents that can be used to uplift, uphold, and empower *this group.*

Thank you for stirring me to become part of *this group.*

Thank you that *this group* can be part of your eternal plan.

LISTENING

Again, I tell you that if two of you on earth agree about anything you ask for, it will be done for you by my Father in heaven. For where two or three come together in my name, there am I with them.

MATTHEW 18:19-20

RETURNING

Recall the image of the single tree in the expansive field. Now imagine other trees growing around it until a small thicket forms. See the beauty in this thicket—the different varieties of leaves and berries on the trees. Realize that just as there are many varieties of trees, so there are many varieties of people and particular gifts in your group.

A QUIET

SPACE

to Celebrate

Special

Occasions

Celebrating
Someone's Birthday

CALMING

From birth I have relied on you;
    you brought me forth from my mother's
      womb.
I will ever praise you.

PSALM 71:6

CENTERING

Think of the person whose birthday you are celebrating. Imagine this person sitting at a table. In front of *him/her* is a large gift. Slowly *he/she* begins to open the gift, removing the shiny satin ribbon, lifting the lid, and pulling back the layers of tissue paper.

PRAYING

It's *this person's* birthday today, O God.

I celebrate this day because *he/she* is so special in my life. As I think about *him/her* and the times we have shared, I am so grateful that *he/she* was born. I can't imagine what my life would have been like if *this person* hadn't been born.

Thank you, God, for *this person.*

I hold *him/her* up to you on this special day and pray that you will lay your loving hand on *this person,* wrap *him/her* in the spirit of your love, and cover *him/her* with the cloak of your concern. Give *him/her* the knowledge of your presence and caring. I pray, God, that on *this person's* birthday, you are with *him/her* every moment, letting *him/her* know that *he/she* is your child and that you celebrate *his/her* day with *him/her.*

On *this person's birthday,* Loving God, I ask that you give *him/her* the special gift of yourself.

Let *him/her* feel your presence so near,
    so real,
        and so palpable
            that *he/she* will have no doubt that
                you are with *him/her.*

Today, O God, turn *his/her* every moment, every thought, and every breath toward you.

I thank you, God, for *this person.*

I thank you for *his/her* part in my life.

I thank you for giving *him/her* the ultimate gift: the gift of salvation.

LISTENING

Now this is eternal life: that they may know you, the only true God, and Jesus Christ, whom you have sent.

JOHN 17:3

RETURNING

Throughout the day, continue to imagine *this person* opening the wonderful gift and feeling the incredible presence of Jesus with *him/her.*

Celebrating
an Anniversary

CALMING
I remember the days of long ago;
I meditate on all your works
and consider what your hands have done.

PSALM 143:5

CENTERING
Remember *this event* whose anniversary you are celebrating. Try to remember the colors, the sounds, the smells, and the sights around you. Relive the feelings of that moment. Enjoy being there once again.

PRAYING
Today is the anniversary of *this event*, O God.
So many things have happened between that

day and this, and yet I still remember it clearly.

I thank you for what *this event* was, for what it meant then and for what it means now.

I thank you for how *this event* changed all the events that followed it.

At the time, I didn't know what would happen afterward. I just enjoyed *this event* for the feelings and moments surrounding it. Now as I celebrate the anniversary of *this event,* I realize that *this event* is part of me:

> who I am,
>> where I am,
>>> how I am,
>>>> why I am.

Just as you have done with so many things in my life, O God, you took *this event* and used it to transform me into the person you wanted me to be.

I thank you that *this event* happened in my life. I thank you for the promise that was in it. I thank you for the time between then and now and for all the emotions, thoughts, and feelings during that time.

Thank you for using all of the events in my life, whether I remember them as an anniversary or let them slip by.

This event is important to me, O God. As I think about it, I once again see your promise that all things work together for good.

LISTENING
Do you have eyes but fail to see, and ears but fail to hear? And don't you remember?

MARK 8:18

RETURNING
Continue to think about *this event*. Explore all the aspects of that day, and see how they have contributed to making the person you are today. Thank God for using all the events of your life to create the person God wants you to become.

Celebrating
Your Birthday

CALMING

My frame was not hidden from you
   when I was made in the secret place.
When I was woven together in the depths of the
   earth,
   your eyes saw my unformed body.
All the days ordained for me
   were written in your book
   before one of them came to be.

PSALM 139:15-16

CENTERING

In your mind, imagine a pile of gifts, all covered
in bright wrapping paper and tied with ribbons.

161

Loving God, this is a special day for me. It's also a day of accounting as I realize that another year has passed. I am another year older.

What have I accomplished? How have I made my world a better place? How have I been faithful to your calling?

(Recall the past year and its events.)

These are the milestones of this past year, O God. Thank you for being with me.

And in the times that might not have been milestones but were just part of the fabric of my life, you were also with me:

times of joy,
> times of sorrow;

in my laughter, in my tears,
> and even in my anger;

in my battles and my victories.
> You were always with me.

How wonderful it is to realize that this year has been a year I've spent with you. Thank you, God, for the gift of this past year.

Now I thank you for the gift of the coming year. Help me to enjoy it, to share it, and to cherish it. It is a gift from you.

LISTENING

You did not choose me, but I chose you and appointed you to go and bear fruit—fruit that will last.

JOHN 15:16

RETURNING

Take a moment to think of the coming year. Imagine that you are opening all the packages on the table in front of you. Inside are the gifts the Spirit makes available to you: wisdom, knowledge, faith, healing, miracles, prophecy, discernment.

Celebrating a Wedding

CALMING

They are led in with joy and gladness;
   they enter the palace of the king.

PSALM 45:15

CENTERING

Think about a simple gold ring and the never-ending circle the ring makes.

PRAYING

Gracious God, this is a day of special joy and celebration as *this person* and *this person* are united in marriage.

I am so happy for them. I thank you that they found each other.

Thank you for the commitment they are making to each other and to you.

Thank you for this day and all the joy it brings to so many people.

O God, I lift up *this person* and *this person* to you. Be with them in their life together. Marriage can be a difficult path sometimes. I ask you to stand as a buffer between these two people. In this way, everything they say, feel, or think about each other will be filtered through you and your love.

As they make their vows this day, be with them and create a threefold cord with them. Let this cord—between *this person* and *this person* and you—endure through the years with the love and joy of this day.

As they make their vows this day, make them aware of your presence. Lead them to realize that you are part of their bond to each other.

Give them joy.

Deepen their love.

Strengthen their union.

Bring them closer to you.

Thank you, O God, that they are now part of each other's lives and part of your greater plan.

Listening

So they are no longer two, but one flesh. Therefore, what God has joined together, let no one separate.

MATTHEW 19:6, NRSV

Returning

Throughout the day, as you think of this couple, continue to see the golden ring as a symbol of their marriage: made of a strong metal, shining in the light, a never-ending circle of eternal love.

Celebrating
a Confirmation

CALMING

Guide me in your truth and teach me,
   for you are God my Savior,
and my hope is in you all day long.

PSALM 25:5

CENTERING

Bring to mind the face of the person being confirmed. Take a moment to see *him/her* clearly. Then imagine a beautiful white dove fluttering above *his/her* head. Imagine light pouring down from the dove—pouring over the person being confirmed. Hold this image of the flowing light in your mind.

O Lamb of God, I thank you that *this person* is publicly announcing the decision to become your follower. This is a momentous time in *his/her* spiritual life, a time when the Holy Spirit's promise is fulfilled.

As *this person* makes *his/her* vows of confirmation, may *he/she* be fully aware of what *he/she* is promising.

As *he/she* stands before the altar and promises
to renounce Satan,
to follow you,
and to become part of the
church fellowship,
pour your Holy Spirit upon *him/her.*

May *he/she* feel a new dimension open within *his/her* soul.

May *he/she* be aware of the Holy Spirit's presence within *him/her.*

May *he/she* enjoy the promise of that Spirit for the rest of *his/her* life.

Lord Jesus, be with *this person* in a real and tangible way. Let this day mark the beginning of *his/her* walk with you. Let it be the time *he/she* looks back to as the moment when the Holy Spirit became a real presence in *his/her* life.

I thank you, Lord, for *this person* and *his/her* witness to you today. Welcome *him/her* to the fellowship of all your followers as we welcome *him/her* into the church. Give *him/her* the power and grace to continue to walk the path you have set for *him/her*.

Dear Jesus, I also ask you to make this day a special one for all the people taking part in this celebration: the families, the congregation, the ministers, the choir. Touch each of them in some way. Remind them of their own confirmation and of the Holy Spirit that now lives within them.

Thank you, Jesus, for the Comforter, the Holy Spirit. Thank you for fulfilling that promise in us when we affirm our faith in you and promise to walk in your ways.

LISTENING

I will ask the Father, and he will give you another Counselor to be with you forever—the Spirit of truth. The world cannot accept him, because it neither sees him nor knows him. But you know him, for he lives with you and will be in you.

JOHN 14:16-17

Returning

As you think of *this person* and *his/her* confirmation, continue to imagine the golden light from the Holy Spirit pouring down on *him/her.* Close your eyes and see *this person* infused with the Holy Spirit of God.

Celebrating
a Baptism

CALMING
I am under vows to you, O God;
   I will present my thank offerings to you.

PSALM 56:12

CENTERING
Imagine a waterfall—clear, sparkling, flowing—a never-ending cascade of water. Hear the sound of the waterfall in your mind.

PRAYING
Baptisms bring me mixed emotions, dear Jesus. I feel joy for the young child being brought to you or for the person affirming a decision to follow you. I also feel sorrow over how lightly some people make the promises of baptism.

The parents make promises on behalf of their child.

The godparents make promises to the child.

The congregation makes promises to the child.

An adult or young person makes promises on his or her own behalf.

Everyone makes promises. Promises are part of the ritual.

I wonder, Does anyone stop to think about what he or she is promising to do? Does the congregation make a concerted effort to keep this child in the church? Do the parents fulfill their promise to bring the child to church regularly? Do the godparents offer spiritual guidance to the child? Does the adult continue to grow and mature in the Christian faith? Sometimes, but not always.

Where did baptism lose its significance, Lord Jesus? Your own baptism was an important event in your life—so important that God voiced approval from the heavens.

Today, Jesus, I pray that this baptism will be different. I pray that this service will have deep significance to all who take part in it. I pray that everyone will be aware of your presence.

I thank you for *this person* who is being

brought into the fellowship today. As the water is poured or sprinkled upon or over *him/her,* may it symbolize your ever-flowing love. From that moment on, may *this person* always be aware of your presence.

I pray that you will pour that same ever-flowing love on everyone who takes part in this service. Help each person realize the importance of this particular moment, not only in the life of *this person* but also in their own lives. As they renew their own vows of baptism, let this become a new moment with you. Refresh their faith, refill their spirit, and restore their joy.

LISTENING

Whoever believes and is baptized will be saved, but whoever does not believe will be condemned.

MARK 16:16

RETURNING

Continue to think about the ever-flowing, clear, sparkling waterfall. See it as a representation of God's love flowing over, through, and around every person involved in the baptism ceremony.

Celebrating
Christmas

CALMING

When I look at your heavens,
   the work of your fingers,
the moon and the stars that you have
   established,
what are human beings that you
   are mindful of them,
mortals that you care for them?

PSALM 8:3-4, NRSV

CENTERING

Imagine standing alone on a hillside at night. The sky is filled with stars. Suddenly one star glows brightly, increasing in radiance until you feel bathed in its light. With this starlight comes a profound sense of peace and joy.

PRAYING

Christmas is such a wonderful time, Jesus, when we celebrate your birth into our dark world.

Christmas is also a difficult time. Many people don't have the trappings of the season: the family, the feasting, the gifts, the social whirl.

It's difficult, Jesus, when I suddenly discover that I'm just like everyone else:

> rushing,
>> finding,
>>> doing,
>>>> eating,
>>>>> drinking,

and forgetting why I celebrate Christmas.

It's difficult because everything around me pushes me into the Christmas of this world.

Even at church I feel a sense of rushing that has nothing in common with the peace and serenity of Christmas.

The Sunday school pageant,
> the Christmas bazaar,
>> the choir concerts,
>>> the special services,

all hurl me toward Christmas Day.

Then when the day finally arrives, I'm too tired to think about the reason I'm celebrating.

Once the presents have been unwrapped, food has been devoured, and families have been duly visited, not much time remains for you.

And so, Jesus, I'm asking you for a special gift as I celebrate your birth: Pour down the light of your star in the East. Bathe me in its peaceful light so that I can experience profound joy, which comes from knowing that my Savior is born. Blessed Jesus, keep me in your peace, today and always.

LISTENING

I have come that they may have life, and have it to the full.

JOHN 10:10

RETURNING

As you prepare for Christmas Day, every time you feel yourself beginning to get caught up in this world's Christmas or beginning to feel stressed or hurried, take a moment to close your eyes briefly and remember the beautiful, brightly shining star. Allow its light to pour down upon you. Feel the peace, experience the joy, and celebrate the birth of your Savior.

Celebrating
Easter

CALMING

They rise in the darkness as a light for the
upright;

    they are gracious, merciful, and righteous.

PSALM 112:4, NRSV

CENTERING

Think of a place outside where you like to be.
Imagine that you are there just before dawn.
The world is hushed and still. Then imagine
that the sky begins to lighten, birds begin to
sing, and soft breezes begin to ruffle the leaves
on the trees. Stand still for moment, enjoying
the dawning of a new day.

This is the day, O Christ. This is the dawning of the Christian faith.

I often think about Mary wandering through the garden at dawn that first Easter morning. She must have felt desolate, alone, devastated by the events of the previous two days. I often wonder how she was able to cope with it:

the crushing disappointment,

the end to all her dreams and desires,

the despair,

the grief.

Did she come to the garden for a last farewell?

Did she plan to return to the life she knew before she met you?

I think I know how Mary felt when she saw that the tomb was empty and you were gone. I've felt that way sometimes—so despairing and so alone. Life piles up on me and I wander through the garden, looking for you. But then, like Mary, I hear your voice calling me, and I know that no matter what happens,

no matter what I've done,

no matter where I've been

or where I go,

you are there!

And always, dear Christ, all I need to do is to answer you, to offer myself to you in prayer. Then, just like the miracle of that first Easter morning, you are there. You are always there.

Every day in my life is Easter because every day you, Jesus Christ, the risen Lord, are with me. At the dawning of each new day, I know that what lies ahead is part of your plan for me and that you are with me.

LISTENING

Woman, . . . why are you crying? Who is it you are looking for?

JOHN 20:15

RETURNING

Throughout the day let yourself briefly experience the dawn. For just a moment, close your eyes. See the sun begin to rise over the darkened earth, and thank God for Jesus' resurrection.

Celebrating
New Year's Day

❧

Calming

Create in me a pure heart, O God,
   and renew a steadfast spirit within me.

PSALM 51:10

Centering

Imagine a sheet of paper, blank except for the numbers of this year written at the top. Sit quietly as you see this sheet of paper in your mind. It is clean, white, and unmarked.

Praying

How the years fly by, Ever-present God. I look at this year's date, and not long ago it seemed impossible that this year would come, that I would still be around. It's not that I didn't think

I would live this long; it's just that this year seemed so far away. And now it's here.

The years do seem to pass more quickly now. It seems that just yesterday was last New Year's Day, and only a week before that was the previous New Year's Day.

Most people think of New Year's Day as a day of beginnings. They wipe the slate clean, look forward, and begin again. Dear God, I see New Year's Day as an opportunity to look back on the slate and then begin again.

And so, I look back on this past year:
the good times and bad times,
the joy and the sorrow,
the changes,
the life transitions,
and the same old,
same old . . .

At times I have felt very close to you, O God.

And at other times I have felt far away.

But in all these times, I know that you were with me.

Now I begin to look to the year ahead. I see these twelve months, these fifty-two weeks, these three hundred sixty-five days as endless, unlimited possibilities with you.

I put this year into your hands. Only you, O God, know what lies ahead. You know the challenges, the joys, and the sorrows. I give you the blank page of this year of my life.

In this new year, help me to obey your will, listen to your voice, and walk in your path.

I thank you, O God, for this year.

I thank you for all we will do together.

I thank you for all you will do through me.

I thank you for all that will be done to me through you.

Thank you, O God, for this year.

LISTENING

The Spirit of the Lord is on me,
    because he has anointed me
    to preach good news to the poor.
He has sent me to proclaim
    freedom for the prisoners
    and recovery of sight for the blind,
to release the oppressed,
    to proclaim the year of the Lord's favor.

LUKE 4:18-19

Returning

See again the blank page representing this year. Realize that what goes on that page is up to you: whether you will serve God or serve this world. Give thanks that this year is part of God's plan for you.

A QUIET
SPACE
for Endings
and
Beginnings

When You
Want to Pray for Healing

CALMING

[God] sent forth his word and healed them;
  he rescued them from the grave.

PSALM 107:20

CENTERING

Picture the person for whom you are praying. If you know the specific health concern—for example, a heart problem—focus on the related area of the person's body. If praying for yourself, target the area of your body that needs healing.

PRAYING

O Great Physician, I lift up *this person* to you. These things I know, Lord Jesus:

  I know that you love *this person/me.*

- I know that you have the power to heal all our afflictions.
- I know that you never turned away anyone who came to you for healing.
- I know that all things work together for good and that you can use even this affliction for your glory.

I know all these things, and still I hesitate to ask you for healing.

Am I afraid I'm being presumptuous by assuming that healing is part of your plan? Or am I afraid I won't see your answer to my prayer? Or that I won't like the answer that I receive?

Or am I afraid you won't answer me at all?

These things I know, Lord Jesus:

- I know that you love *this person/me.*
- I know that you hear my prayers.
- I know that you answer my prayers.

So why do I still hesitate?

Perhaps it's because I don't see much of your healing power around me. So many people need your healing touch. They pray for a healing that I don't see happening. They talk about an inner healing, yet that's not what they prayed for.

So I hesitate.

These things I know, Lord Jesus:

- I know that you love *this person/me.*
- I know that you healed the blind, made the lame to walk, and gave peace to the afflicted.
- I know that you overcame death.

Because I know these things, Jesus, I will hesitate no longer. Standing upon the firm foundation of what I know to be true, I ask you to put your healing hand upon *this person/me.* I ask you to touch what hurts, heal what is broken, and restore what is lost.

I ask this, Jesus, with the small seed of faith that I have: faith in what I know to be true.

LISTENING

Daughter, your faith has healed you. Go in peace.

LUKE 8:48

RETURNING

Continue to concentrate on the area that needs healing. Imagine that the area begins to glow with an inward heat, and picture the love of Jesus penetrating and touching all of the area. See the area glowing with the light of healing. Picture it healed and whole. Throughout the day, continue to envision this healing process taking place.

When You
Need Forgiveness

CALMING

Then I acknowledged my sin to you
and did not cover up my iniquity.
I said, "I will confess
my transgressions to the LORD"—
and you forgave
the guilt of my sin.

PSALM 32:5

CENTERING

Imagine that you stand facing a long wooden
board fence. The fence boards are nailed closely
together so you can't see between them. You
can't see over the fence, and you can't see its end.

I'm sorry, God. I don't know what else to say. I'm sorry.

It shouldn't have happened. I shouldn't have done it. I'm sorry.

I knew it was wrong, but I did it anyway. I guess I thought it wouldn't really matter—that what I did wouldn't make much of a difference in the larger scheme of things. But now I realize that it has made a great difference—especially in our relationship.

My sin stands between us, God, like a fence between neighboring backyards. We can talk over the fence, we can even see each other, but we can't touch. That's what I miss most: the sense of being in touch with you.

I've tried reaching over the fence. That didn't work very well.

I've tried walking around the fence, but it has no end.

I've tried ignoring the fence, but it seems to grow longer every day. I'm beginning to think that I'm stuck with that fence, God.

I didn't realize that a fence could be built so easily or so quickly. One day, it was a single board, that one small thing that I shouldn't have done. Now more boards are added daily to the fence as I try to cover up, to forget, to ignore that first board. I don't know where it will end.

I don't want to continue living like this, dear God, with a fence between us—a fence of my own building.

O God, I'm truly sorry for what I did, and I'm asking you to forgive me. Tear down this fence with the power of your forgiveness. Let me see you fully, face-to-face; let me speak to you with nothing else between us.

Dear Lord, I ask you to remove any other fences I may have built inadvertently with this one thing I should not have done—fences between me and others, fences between persons who don't know that I was the one who put up the first board.

Restore us all to you, O God.

Forgive me.

LISTENING

Therefore, I tell you, her sins, which were many, have been forgiven; hence she has shown great love. But the one to whom little is forgiven, loves little.

LUKE 7:47, NRSV

Returning

Close your eyes and imagine the long board fence. Now imagine a silent whirlwind blowing down the length of the fence, ripping up the boards and flinging them up into the sky, where they soon disappear. See this powerful, silent wind blowing away the entire fence until nothing remains.

When You
Need Guidance

CALMING

I will instruct you and teach you in the way you
    should go;
I will counsel you and watch over you.

PSALM 32:8

CENTERING

Imagine that you are walking down a long hallway. Doors line both sides of the hallway, and
all of them are closed. The outside of the doors
do not indicate where they lead or what lies behind them.

PRAYING

I have so many choices facing me right now,
Guiding God. I don't want to make the wrong

one. I want to make the choice that you want me to make, but I can't seem to figure out which one that is. All the choices look good to me.

They all have possibilities.

They all have enticing aspects.

All offer good reasons to choose them.

So I'm stuck here, trying to make a decision, trying to decide which is the right choice for me, trying to stay within your will.

I need your guidance, God. I need to hear your voice and feel your touch. I need to know that my choice is the one you want for me.

In the silence I lift up all the possibilities to you. *(Think of the different options for which you are seeking guidance.)*

In the silence I let go of all of these possibilities. I release them so that your guidance will be clear to me, unhampered by my own desires.

In the silence, O God, I listen for your voice.

I listen with an open heart. I trust that you will guide me to the right choice. In this trusting, I am going to move out in faith and open the doors in front of me.

If I try to open the wrong door, Guiding God, keep it tightly closed and locked. If I try the right door, let it swing open easily. Let the entrance be wide and the road open on the other side. This is how I will know that I've found the right door.

Ever-present God, the process of opening doors begins now. Please help me discern the best choice.

LISTENING

When he, the Spirit of truth, comes, he will guide you into all truth. He will not speak on his own; he will speak only what he hears, and he will tell you what is yet to come.

JOHN 16:13

RETURNING

In your mind's eye, begin to move down the hallway, trying the doors on either side. Only one door will open; the others resist any attempts to force them open. See yourself opening that door and walking through the doorway.

When You Need Freedom from an Addiction

CALMING

In my anguish I cried to the LORD,
   and he answered by setting me free.

PSALM 118:5

CENTERING

Imagine a thick, heavy chain wrapped around your body. Feel its weight on your shoulders, the tightness of the cold metal. Imagine trying to move with this chain around you.

PRAYING

Set me free, Jesus!
   Set me free, Jesus!

Set me free from *this addiction.*

Day and night I fight against it. Every waking moment, every dream, every breath, every heartbeat, every thought—every part of me is chained to this addiction.

Release my bondage, Jesus.

Release my bondage, Jesus.

Release me from bondage to *this addiction.*

So often I've believed I was free. But always, again and again, the chains returned, each time heavier and tighter than the time before.

Loose me now, Jesus.

Loose me now, Jesus.

Loose me from *this addiction's* chains.

In my pride I thought I could do it by myself. I thought that my self-control was stronger than *this addiction.* I believed that if only I tried harder, I would be free.

Take my burden, Jesus.

Take my burden, Jesus.

Take my burden of *this addiction.*

Now I come to you, Jesus. I am defeated, beaten, bound, and chained. I have no place else to go, no one else to turn to but to you.

Accept my prayer, Jesus.

Accept my prayer, Jesus.

Accept my prayer about *this addiction.*
I can do nothing more about *this addiction.*
Set me free. Loose my bondage. Release me
now. Take my burden. Accept my prayer.

Listening
If the Son sets you free, you will be free indeed.

JOHN 8:36

Returning
Imagine that the chain binding you suddenly
falls, dropping into a heap around your feet. Step
over it and feel the lightness in your body. Lift
your arms and turn around in perfect freedom.
When you feel the need for *this addiction,* visualize the chain falling from your body. Remind
yourself that you are now free to step away.

When You
Seek a New Walk
with the Lord

CALMING

You have made known to me the path of life;
   you will fill me with joy in your presence,
   with eternal pleasures at your right hand.

PSALM 16:11

CENTERING

Imagine walking down a broad, well-traveled road. Other people are walking on the road, but you are alone. As you walk along, you see other smaller roads branching off the main road, some overgrown, some equally well-traveled, some little more than tracks leading off into the distance. You don't see anyone on those roads.

It's not that I dislike the road I'm on with you, dear Jesus. It's a good road—broad, smooth, easy to navigate. Perhaps it's too easy.

I've gotten used to this road. I know most of its little curves and bumps, its small hills and rough patches. I've walked on it for a long time.

But now I'm starting to look at the other roads that lead from this one. I've never really noticed them before because I've been too busy concentrating on walking on this road, one foot in front of the other, one mile after another.

Now that walking doesn't take all my concentration, I find myself looking for other routes—routes that might offer me a few challenges, surprises, and new vistas.

It's not that I'm bored with this road, Lord Jesus. I know it's the road that you chose for me when we first started out on this journey together, and I wasn't very sure of my footing.

I'm just wondering if this feeling I have is your way of telling me to look around me, look at the other roads you have for your followers.

Jesus, I'd like to walk with you down some of those other roads. I'd like to explore some new pathways and find some new horizons.

Show me the way you want me to go.
Bring me to new perspectives of you,
new experiences with your Holy Spirit,
new hills and valleys of belief,
new streams of living water,
new joys and sorrows.

Deepen my experience of you as we walk down this new road together, Jesus. Show me where I must step out boldly on my own, where I must cut through the undergrowth of my old ways and thoughts to find the new pathways that await me.

I feel such anticipation as I sit here in the silence, knowing that you have heard my prayer and that you are, even now, waiting for me to begin our new journey together.

LISTENING

Enter through the narrow gate. For wide is the gate and broad is the road that leads to destruction, and many enter through it. But small is the gate and narrow the road that leads to life, and only a few find it.

MATTHEW 7:13-14

Returning

Imagine stopping in the middle of that broad road. Picture yourself looking to the left and right, seeing the roads, paths, and trails on each side. Imagine turning toward one of them and then taking the first step off the broad road.

When
Someone You Love Dies

Calming

Even though I walk
 through the valley of the shadow of death,
I will fear no evil,
 for you are with me;
your rod and your staff,
 they comfort me.

Psalm 23:4

Centering

Imagine sitting in a beautiful garden, enclosed by a high brick wall. You can see the sky overhead, but you can't see beyond the brick wall. In the brick wall is an open door. Beyond it, you see a wonderful vista of rolling hills. The door slowly closes. Sit in the garden for a moment.

PRAYING

O God of all comfort, I miss *this person*. I miss *him/her* so much.

As I sit here, there is a vacuum in my world, an empty space that *he/she* once occupied. I feel that empty space. The talk, the laughter, the many things we shared together—all of these have ended. And only the empty space remains.

How I wish that I could turn back the clock. I wish that I could go back to a time when we were together, happy and carefree. If only I'd known how little time we would have together. I would have treasured each minute, each second. Instead, I let it slip by.

I can't change time. I can only go on from here, seeing the time that stretches ahead of me, without *this person*.

How can I bear it?

> Already the days are long,
>> the hours drag by,
>>> the minutes are endless,
>>>> without *this person*.

Dear God, come to me now. Fill this empty space with your love and your grace. Be with me in the days and months and years to come. Help me to live in this world without *this person*.

Ease my aching heart with your gentle touch, O God, so that the pain lessens, the longing ceases, and the sorrow lightens. Let me feel your presence with me every moment of the time to come. In my grief, dear God, let me know that eventually joy will come in the morning.

There is joy in these moments as I thank you for *this person.*

Thank you for all *he/she* has meant to me.

Thank you for the impact *he/she* has made on the lives of others.

Thank you for *his/her* life.

Thank you that in the time of *his/her* death, I can come to you for comfort.

And now, dear God, as I begin my journey without *this person,* I trust that you will be with me. Help me to rest in your unchanging love.

Listening

I am the resurrection and the life. Those who believe in me, even though they die, will live, and everyone who lives and believes in me will never die.

John 11:25, NRSV

RETURNING

Sit quietly in your beautiful imaginary garden. Think of *this person* as being on the other side of the door, enjoying the new landscape that lies beyond the brick wall. Remember that one day you also will go through the door and join *him/her.*

When
a Special Time Ends

CALMING

They will perish, but you remain;
   they will all wear out like a garment.
Like clothing you will change them
   and they will be discarded.
But you remain the same,
   and your years will never end.

PSALM 102:26-27

CENTERING

Find a symbol for your special time—something you can hold in your hand. For example, if you've vacationed at the beach, your symbol might be a shell. If you've spent time with your mother, your symbol might be a piece of jewelry she has given you. When you have chosen your symbol, hold it for a few minutes.

PRAYING

I wish this time didn't have to end, O God. I've been so happy and enjoyed myself so much. It's hard to let it go and move on.

But I have no choice.

Your universe continually moves on,
> from endings to beginnings,
>> to endings and beginnings again.

This ending is just part of that universe.

No doubt this ending is part of your plan for me within this universe. It doesn't seem like a good part of the plan, but only you know what beginning this ending signals.

Although I feel heavyhearted and sad as I say good-bye to a time in my life that seems so promising and rich, I trust you. Whatever lies ahead of me, I know that you are with me.

Perhaps the road ahead is simply more of the same road I have traveled before this special time. Lift me from boredom and letdown.

The road may lead to a new mountain I have never climbed before. Hold me and sustain me in the hard places.

The road may lead to a deep valley, dark and shadowed. Walk with me, dear God, and give me comfort.

Always let me look back on this special time as a space of joy and delight in my life, free from regret and sorrow. Let its memory be a haven for me, like the special places I remember from my childhood.

Take away any bitterness I may feel at this ending, O God. Fill my heart with thanksgiving and joy that you have given me the gift of this special time.

Listening

No one sews a piece of unshrunk cloth on an old cloak, for the patch pulls away from the cloak, and a worse tear is made. Neither is new wine put into old wineskins; otherwise, the skins burst, and the wine is spilled, and the skins are destroyed; but new wine is put into fresh wineskins, and so both are preserved.

Matthew 9:16-17, nrsv

Returning

Hold your symbol of the special time close to you. Then imagine carefully placing it into a small box. Put the lid on. Know that the box is there, ready for you to open and remember your special time.

When a Relationship Breaks Down

♨

CALMING

Turn to me and be gracious to me,
    for I am lonely and afflicted.
The troubles of my heart have multiplied;
    free me from my anguish.

PSALM 25:16

CENTERING

Imagine that you are standing on the top of a high hill and looking at the distant landscape. A gentle wind blows. Enjoy the sense of freedom and release.

PRAYING

I've tried everything, Lord Jesus.
    I've tried reaching out.

I've tried drawing back.

I've tried talking.

I've tried silence.

I've cried, pleaded, yelled, and whispered.

I've prayed.

I can't think of anything else to do.

So I give this relationship to you. I ask for nothing—no special favors, no divine interventions, no sudden revelations. I simply place the relationship in your hands.

And in giving it to you, I feel great relief. It is done. I have finally given up and accepted this ending. I know that from this moment on, my life will be different, and I accept this beginning as well.

Give me the strength to let all else go. Keep me from returning to my strivings to maintain *this relationship*. Remind me that I have given it to you.

Lead me to the higher ground, dear Jesus, where I can leave behind any bitterness, accusations, anger, sorrow, and pain. Fill me instead with your peace and the knowledge that you are with me.

Be in this space between the ending and the beginning. It is a scary place for me as I begin to work through my life without *this relationship* in it. Be between what was—the memories, the dreams, and the hopes—and what is to come.

Draw me closer to you in this time between the ending and the beginning. Let me see the place ahead not as a place to be feared but as a place you have prepared for me.

LISTENING

I am the light of the world. Whoever follows me will never walk in darkness, but will have the light of life.

JOHN 8:12

RETURNING

Continue to imagine yourself atop the windy hill. Realize that the climb is over and now you are free to go in any direction you choose. Enjoy the cleansing wind blowing around you. Enjoy the feeling of anticipation for the road ahead.

About the Author

Known for her down-to-earth style and remarkable candor, Patricia Wilson conducts more than one hundred business seminars across Canada and the United States annually, specializing in interpersonal communication topics. She is also the best-selling author of seven nonfiction books published by The Upper Room.

Patricia is a graduate of Ryerson University in Toronto, Canada. She is a teacher, educator, and marketing expert who has worked as a technical writer, editor, and layout artist. For the past ten years she has been executive director of her own company, Life Track, which provides training for secular and Christian groups. Most recently, Patricia founded Deeper Waters, an organization that offers Christian seminars and workshops to church and service organizations.

Patricia is active in her local church congregation and is a licensed lay reader. She and her husband, Gerald, have three grown children and live on an island off the coast of Nova Scotia.

Personal
Reflections

Use the remaining pages to record insights or other thoughts that come to you during prayer times.